THE ART
AND CRAFT OF
QUILTING

THE ART AND CRAFT OF QUILTING

A Beginner's Guide to Patchwork Design, Color, and Expression

Daisy Grubbs

WATSON-GUPTILL PUBLICATIONS/NEW YORK

Page 1:
WHAT SIZE IS A RABBIT'S HOLE?
by Christine Adams.
Photo by Ronnie Haber.

Page 2:
FEATURING THE VIOLETS
by Jeanne Benson.
Photo by Mark Gulezian.

Page 5:
WASHINGTON SQUARE II
by Christine Adams.
Photo by Breger and Assoc., Inc.

Page 6:
STAR STEPS
by Dorothy Holden.
Photo by Joseph E. Garland.

Daisy Grubbs first came to national attention when her earthenware, stoneware, and porcelain portraits were featured in *American Artist* magazine (January 1980). Her book, *Modeling a Likeness in Clay,* which was published by Watson-Guptill in 1982, is still the standard reference on the subject.

The mother of seven children, Ms. Grubbs has maintained a studio in her home for thirty-five years. When her career as a sculptor was brought to a halt by a back injury, her modeling tools and blocks of clay were replaced by pastels and paints. Her studio was transformed once more when she created a memorial quilt for her son, Charles Halstrick. The resulting work, a magnificent triptych featured in the last chapter, reflects her background in painting and sculpture.

Daisy Grubbs's work has been represented by several galleries, and she has taught workshops around the United States.

Senior Editor: Candace Raney
Edited by Joy Aquilino
Designed by Bob Fillie, Graphiti Graphics
Graphic production by Ellen Greene

First published in 1995 in the United States
by Watson-Guptill Publications,
a division of BPI Communications, Inc.,
1515 Broadway, New York, N.Y. 10036

Library of Congress Cataloging-in-Publication Data
Grubbs, Daisy.
    The art and craft of quilting: a beginner's guide to patchwork
design, color, and expression / Daisy Grubbs.
        p.   cm.
    Includes bibliographical references and index.
    ISBN 0-8230-4494-7
    1. Patchwork—patterns. 2. Quilting. 3. Quilts. I. Title.
TT835.G78   1995
746.46—dc20   94-42987
                                           CIP

Manufactured in Malaysia

First printing, 1995

1 2 3 4 5 6 7 8 9 / 03 02 01 00 99 98 97 96 95

To my son
Charles Alan Halstrick
1955–1987

ACKNOWLEDGMENTS

The enthusiastic response to my work of the members of the Unitarian Universalist Church of Silver Spring, Maryland, inspired me to write this book.

Alice Pritchard, friend and colleague, spent countless hours reading the manuscript with a critical eye. Her comments and suggestions were invaluable, as were those of my daughter, Carolyn Pedrick.

In sharing their quilts with my readers, Christine Adams, Jeanne Benson, Katharine Brainard, Sarah Crooke, Ellen Dashner, Dorothy Holden, Susan Johnson, Kai Rim Park, Donna Radner, Nancy Shapiro, Lois Smith, and Michelle Vernon have enriched the book immensely.

Associate editor Joy Aquilino determined the structure for the text, and in a few weeks of intense effort brought about the metamorphosis from manuscript to manual. Bob Fillie's talent for design is evident on every page, and Ellen Greene's expert management of the book's graphic production contributed significantly to its success.

My supportive husband, Don, suffered neglect without complaint so that I could have the time and space to concentrate on getting the job done in accustomed obsessive style.

My gratitude to them all is boundless.

CONTENTS

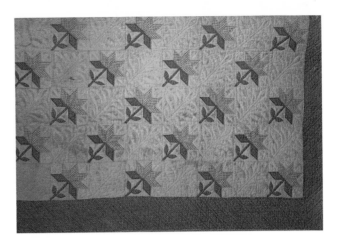

INTRODUCTION

 Victorian confection of lace and velvet ribbons, the quilt of my childhood memories adorns Aunt Margaret's guest bed. It is sixty years ago. I have been tucked in for the night, the ravishing coverlet snug around me. When morning light falls across the bed, I wake to the excitement of exploring that expanse of embellished loveliness. ❧ Today, when designing a quilt of my own, I feel the same excitement. My intention in *The Art and Craft of Quilting* is to share that feeling with you. In our society, which specializes in mass-producing goods, crafters and artists treasure things that are unique or handmade. The more standardized our personal environments become, the greater our hunger for the distinctive, fresh, and original touch.

(Opposite) POPPIES IN THE SAND by Jeanne Benson. 75 × 75 inches.
This quilt, which was made in response to the Gulf War, is machine-appliquéd with decorative stitches.
The quotations embroidered in the corner posts document the symbolic language of war.
(Above) PEONY I (DETAIL) by Julia Amelia Hauser. c. 1857.
This quilt was damaged when it was used to wrap the family silver and
hidden under the corn crib while Sherman's army raided the South.
Courtesy of Virginia Carter Smith, the quilter's great-great-granddaughter.

An assortment of traditional patchwork designs. (Right) A four-patch with border and sashes. (Below left) A nine-patch with border and sashes. (Below center) A hexagon with star points to the sides. (Below right) A hexagon with star points to the corners. (Bottom) A seven-by-seven patch.

WHAT IS QUILTING?

A quilt consists of two layers of fabric between which is inserted a filling (properly called *batting*) intended to provide warmth. Sometimes the top layer is made of many bits of fabric that have been sewn together to make a design. The process of sewing these bits together is called *piecing*. The process of fastening the pieced top to the batting and backing is called *quilting*.

Quilting adds a second layer of linear design on top of the pieced composition and creates a third dimension by causing indentations in the surface. Because the quilting process squeezes the batting down with every stitch, the thicker the batting, the greater the contour. This process also reduces the size of the quilt, so the denser the stitching, the greater the reduction. The density of the stitching should be fairly uniform over the face of the quilt or its shape may be distorted.

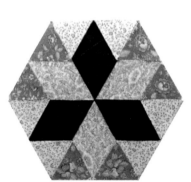

Traditional piecing, as the term implies, uses patterns that have served generations of quilters. Many of these are geometric in style. The One-Patch shown in Chapter 3 is the simplest. Several others are shown on this page. Some designs incorporate *borders,* which frame the composition; *sashes,* which are strips between the squares; and *posts,* which are small squares that connect the sashing strips. Classic geometric patterns can be manipulated in an almost infinite number of ways, giving traditional quilting its perennial fascination.

The term *appliqué* (derived from the French word *appliquer,* "to put on") is used to describe a process of applying a cutout of one fabric to a background of another by various methods. This craft has been practiced all over the world since the invention of fabric. It is now, along with piecing, one of the two most common ways of making a quilt top. In this book it is

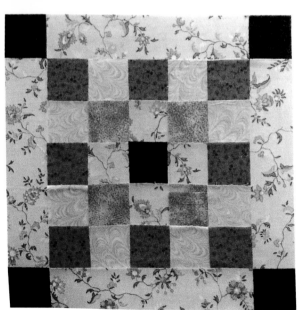

LEAVES
by Kai Rim Park.
1991. 31 × 29 inches.
*This colorful quilt is
a superb example of
machine appliqué by
a master quilter who
is also a fine artist.
Photo by Breger and
Assoc., Inc.*

used to apply letters to a banner, a raised design to a stool top, and images to pillows and a wall hanging.

Also covered are guidelines on creating original quilt designs. I first became aware of the fine art quilt in 1984 when I saw an exhibit at the Textile Museum in Washington, D.C. That show was a thrilling revelation of the possibilities of fabric as a visual medium. Until then I had thought of quiltmaking as a skilled craft of copying antique designs. The contemporary art quilt is a different breed of cat. In the interest of expressing an artistic concept that formerly would have been carried out with pen, pencil, or paint, the art quilt exploits all the characteristics of modern textiles and incorporates such nontextile elements as buttons, sequins, beads, and other lightweight objects.

Beginning with a few examples in the early twentieth century, the quilt as fine art gradually emerged from the American arts and crafts movement, which was an offshoot of the mid–nineteenth century English Arts and Crafts Movement. Quilting found some serious expression on the crest of the

QUILTING STEP-BY-STEP

Before you embark on your first quilting project, it's important to have an idea of the sequence of steps that are part of the process.

- Choose a pattern or develop an image.
- Estimate the yardage needed for each motif.
- Select, prepare, and cut the fabrics.
- Piece the blocks or motifs and/or create the appliqués.
- Set blocks to construct the quilt top (if it is composed of squares).
- Assemble the quilt *sandwich* (quilt top, batting, and backing).
- Layer and baste the quilt.
- Add quilting stitches.
- Bind the quilt.

1960s' wave of interest in handcrafts. In the late 1970s a large corporation decided to decorate its offices with old quilts, siphoning off a major share of the best in the country. As a result of this attention, more people became aware of and learned to appreciate quilts. Demand soared and prices rose steeply. It was inevitable that artists, looking for new ways to express their ideas, would seize upon quilting techniques. The 1980s brought an explosion of activity here and in Europe, applying traditional quilting materials and methods to current aesthetic problems.

HOW TO USE THIS BOOK

Following introductory chapters on materials, techniques, color, and design, the projects in *The Art and Craft of Quilting* begin with traditional quilts and progressively build toward original quilt designs. Even if you've never sewn a stitch before, the first project is well within your grasp. If you're an experienced quilter you'll appreciate the approach to design that evolves from the first quilt through the last. Together they comprise a series of lessons, each

PATTERNS FOR TRADITIONAL PIECED QUILTS

Presented below are fourteen traditional geometric designs, along with hints for their most effective presentation. Each of the templates (see pages 128–141) also includes a piecing sequence diagram.

Dresden Plate
To be effective, this design requires that the four-pointed leaves contrast strongly with the sixteen rounded ones.

Grandmother's Fan
The quarter circle should be dark, the fan blades medium, and the curved piece a solid light-colored fabric.

Grandmother's Flower Garden
Use a bright center hexagon surrounded by six light ones and a final circle of twelve darks.

Tumbling Blocks
You can use any size diamond as a template for these blocks. Always put the darkest diamond in the same position relative to the medium- and light-value ones.

Pinwheel
Use equal numbers of light and dark triangles, either two fabrics or many.

Jacob's Ladder
Five four-patch sections each require a pair of light-value and a pair of medium-value patches. The other four require a light and a dark triangle.

Monkey Wrench
This motif is most effective when only two fabrics are used, one light and one dark.

Kansas Dugout
This design is clear only with a strong light-and-dark contrast. All four sections of the square can be identical or each can use different fabrics as long as the contrast is strong.

Road to California
Use twenty-five medium-value squares, twenty-four light-value triangles, and twenty-four dark triangles.

See Saw
This design uses eight small dark triangles, four small light triangles, four bright large triangles, and four trapezoids in a striking print.

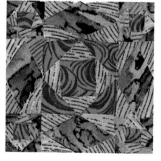

Storm at Sea
Follow the example shown to determine how many of each of the eight templates to cut and how to distribute the values.

Summer Stars
Make the center of the star dark, light, or bright and the surrounding star a contrasting color set against a plain background.

one a little more advanced, that will build your vocabulary of techniques until you have what is needed to conceive and execute your own designs.

The projects in *The Art and Craft of Quilting* offer a swift survey of a dozen kinds of traditional quilts. (On pages 128–141 are templates for fourteen additional patterns, each with a piecing sequence diagram and an example of a completed square. Refer to the box at left for a description of how each pattern can be presented most effectively.) Whether you like traditional patterns or nontraditional composition, you'll find the information on color, line, and shape in the "Color Note" that accompanies each of the projects invaluable.

The best way to learn a skill is to try it. Only with experience can an artist know what problems need to be addressed, at which point instruction becomes most useful. Ideally, an artist approaches a problem intuitively and lets the spirit drive an outward expression of an inner light. For those of us who are not yet free enough to begin with intuition, theory provides a good foundation on which to build creative confidence. In *The Art and Craft of Quilting*, I hope to give you, the quilter and artist, not only the elements of the craft but also a concrete basis for exploring composition with fabric, so that with practice your full range of expression will come into bloom.

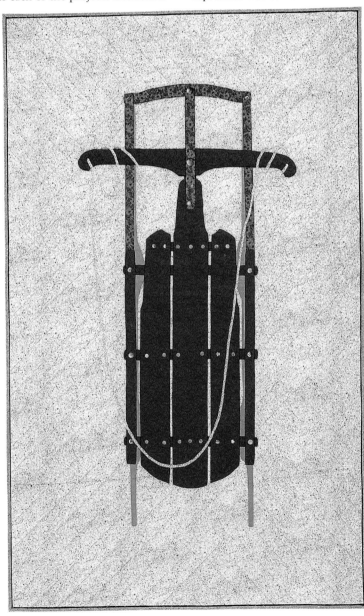

THE FLYER by Jeanne Benson. 40 × 64 inches.
The quilter's family sled, which was first used by her father and then by her and her siblings, was the inspiration for this piece. Photo by Mark Gulezian.

QUILTING BASICS

needle, some thread, scissors, pins, fabric, a comfortable place to sit, and a good light source—these elements are all the great quilters of the past could hope for. Some of their work has survived generations to be treasured by their descendants or displayed in museums around the world. Even if your workspace is as small as a sewing box and a bag of scraps, you can still enjoy the feel of the fabric, the pleasure of combining colors to suit your taste, and the satisfaction of presenting someone you love with the work of your own hands and heart.

(Opposite) AUGUSTA *by Jeanne Benson. 88 × 74 inches.*
The unusually shaped blocks in this quilt were pieced by machine, then quilted by hand.
(Above) In my studio I keep a wide selection of tools and materials, along with the first prize awarded to me by my granddaughter, Meggie.

Tools

There are two major categories of tools for quilters: those that are used to cut fabrics, and those that are used to compose and construct the quilt.

CUTTING TOOLS

In addition to a good pair of sewing shears for cutting curved lines and embroidery scissors for trimming fine details, for a quilter a rotary cutter is indispensable. By positioning the cutting mat beneath your fabric and using a clear plastic ruler as a guide, you can make perfectly straight cuts much more quickly and easily than with scissors. Spread the fabric on your mat, aligning the *grain,* which is the direction of the threads in the weave, with its grid. Press your transparent ruler against the fabric to keep it from slipping. Your rotary cutter will be guided by the edge of the ruler. Keep in mind that the blade will damage easily if you cut across pins or run it against your ruler if it has a metal edge. A nicked blade will leave uncut threads every few inches. Going back and cutting these wastes time.

The surgical steel blade of the Olfa rotary cutter is designed to cut up to sixteen layers of fabric at a time. (Note that the safety shield on its blade does not retract automatically as the Dritz's does.) The advantages of cutting multiple layers of fabrics are that they will all be identical in width and you will save time as well as wear and tear on your hands and your tools.

If you want to try your hand at cutting multiple layers, begin with only two layers, making sure that the grain is carefully aligned. As you gain experience and skill, increase the number of layers to four. To cut four layers, straighten the grain of your fabric, then fold it selvedge to selvedge, then fold once more so that the first fold is on top of the selvedge. Trim the end of the fabric at 90 degrees to the folds using your wide O'Lipfa plastic ruler or T-square as a guide. Cut strips to the widest dimension of the pieces for which you need multiples. Spread these strips out flat, stack them precisely, and cross-cut sets of pieces to the other required dimension. For rectangular pieces, the final cuts are made at right angles to the length of the strips; for

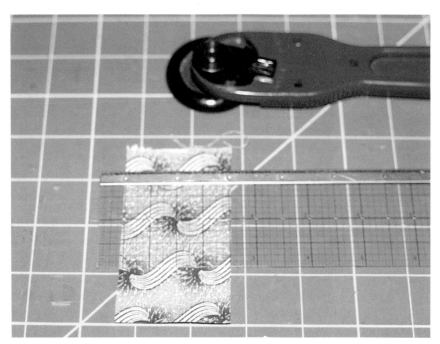

A rotary cutter with its transparent plastic ruler and cutting mat.

triangles or diamonds, they are made on the diagonal.

A clear plastic 12½-inch square and a clear lip-edged ruler about 2 feet by 5 inches that can be used as a T-square, both calibrated precisely, are excellent tools for the serious quilter. Either of these can be used with the rotary cutter. The calibration lines of both are incised on the back, providing traction to keep the fabric from slipping. It is important to use the same rulers throughout a project because the calibrations may differ from ruler to ruler.

TEMPLATES

Templates are stiff patterns that are used to cut many pieces of fabric to the same size and shape. You can use a card stock such as the brightly colored sheets sold in some supermarkets or drug stores for children's school projects. I save old manila file folders for this purpose. Quilting shops sell ready-made plastic templates and sheets of flexible plastic, both clear and translucent, from which you can cut your own. These are less likely to be cut accidentally by your rotary cutter than cardboard ones. Once you've mastered the basic cutting techniques involved in a One-Patch quilt (see Chapter 3), you

should try your hand at some of the patterns at the back of the book, which you can use to make templates for traditional patchwork designs.

PAPER

For your own designing, either of individual templates or of entire quilts, you will need sketching paper to work out the details of each motif. Larger sheets of sketching paper are used to make scale drawings or as a foundation for a *fabric study,* which is a scale model of an entire quilt or of one of its design elements that is made by gluing fabric to a paper backing. Fabric studies are used for a variety of purposes: to determine how a fabric will work within a quilt, to get a clear idea of how much and what kinds of fabrics are necessary for a particular design, or simply to see an idea depicted in fabric before investing time and effort in the actual quilt. Of course, as a quilt is put together unexpected problems do arise, but a fabric study can resolve a multitude of questions before much of the work is done. Note that in addition to the paper you'll need a glue stick to mount the fabric.

Tracing paper, which is used to create overlay grids for enlarging designs, is available in small pads in the stationery section of a supermarket or drugstore. For large-scale works it's better to buy sturdier tracing paper, which is available in large pads and in 36-inch-wide rolls at art supply stores. A large pad of newsprint is useful for making full-size layouts. On occasion I have obtained, free of charge, the ends of rolls of newsprint from one of our local news-papers—a valuable arrangement.

DRAWING, SKETCHING, AND MARKING TOOLS

For marking fabrics for either cutting or piecing, water-erasable pens for light-colored fabrics and silver pencils for dark ones are mandatory additions to your supply list. Ordinary lead pencil is just too difficult to erase from most fabrics. For inscriptions that are meant to endure, such as your signature on the back of a quilt or the text of a poem on the front, a Pigma pen makes a delicate, permanent line.

For sketching and drawing, drawing pencils and a kneaded eraser will do for preliminary sketches, and colored pen-cils, crayons, oil pastels, acrylic paints, and other media will serve to work out color schemes.

SEWING MACHINE

While some quilters believe that piec-ing can be done more accurately and, in the long run, just as quickly if sewn by hand, a simple straight-stitch sewing

machine will do a more than adequate job of piecing. The method you choose will depend on your inclination and your experience; both are equally respectable. Even for the most skilled hand stitcher, using a machine is easier if arthritis is a problem. Satin-stitch and other fancy refinements of the modern sewing machine increase the range of possibilities. Having lots of extra bob-bins can also save time. On a big job you can fill a dozen at once and not have to stop to wind a new one every time one runs out. For machine quilting I use a roller foot which, as its name implies, has rollers that help feed the sandwich smoothly under the needle. If such an attachment is made for your machine, I recommmend that you invest in one. Always have extra sewing machine needles on hand, because there's nothing worse than being caught with a broken needle and no spares after the stores have closed.

NEEDLES AND THIMBLES

For hand piecing your quilt, you'll need quilting needles and thimbles. Quilting needles, which are called *betweens,* have small round eyes that accept quilt-ing thread easily and are shorter than sharps or embroidery needles so they're easier to manipulate for fine sewing. Quilting needles are available in a range of sizes; the larger the number, the finer the needle. I have them in sizes 5 through 10, though I usually use a size

8 for the medium-weight fabrics I tend to work in. On a large quilt like "The Pedricks at Home" (see pages 116–121), I might use as many as six needles at once.

To save wear and tear on my hands, I wear a thimble on both my pushing fin-ger and my receiving finger. The push-ing thimble has a ridge around the top so the needle won't slide off when pres-sure is applied.

IRON AND IRONING BOARD

Your iron and ironing board are impor-tant pieces of equipment. They should be ready at hand so that you can easily press fabric before cutting as well as after sewing each seam before proceed-ing to the next. It's impossible to do accu-rate work without pressing at every stage.

QUILTING FRAME

In the old days a quilting frame was nothing more than four boards tied together to form a rectangle on which to stretch the quilt top, batting, and backing. This simple device might be set on some chairs or hung from ceiling beams. Today there are many different types of quilting frames on the market of varying degrees of complexity and size. Mine is a three-bar frame with ratchets for stretching the quilt and rolling it from end to end as the work proceeds. For a small quilt you might prefer to use a large embroidery hoop either with or without a stand.

A three-bar quilting frame with ratchets.

Materials

Quilts are usually composed of at least three basic elements: fabric, thread, and batting. Within the first two categories lie an almost infinite variety of color, texture, and pattern, but before you begin to explore the creative potential of quilting materials you should understand some aspects of their care and preparation.

THREAD

For machine piecing I use cotton-covered polyester thread, and for hand quilting I recommend Coats Dual Duty Extra-Strong Hand Quilting Thread, which is coated with a resin that prevents it from tangling. As you gain confidence and skill as a quilter and become more adventurous about color and texture, you may want to use embroidery floss, metallic threads, and other embellishments. Keep in mind that due to recent environmental regulations some hues of embroidery floss are no longer colorfast, so you'll have to test them for colorfastness by the method described on the opposite page (see "Preparing Fabrics for Projects").

FABRIC

As with any other medium, fabric has both possibilities and limitations that dictate the form and content of a finished quilt. Fabrics are made with a wide array of physical qualities: coarse, fine, crinkly, velvety, shiny, metallic, transparent, translucent, and opaque. In addition, printed design creates the illusion of texture so that quilters can exploit the creative efforts of textile designers to enhance their compositions. In contrast to many other media, textiles are nontoxic. Quilters don't need to worry about foundry gases, silica dust, turpentine fumes, pastel dust, or the heavy metals found in oil paints. On average, a $1/2$ yard of fabric costs about the same as a tube of oil paint and may contribute to the design of as many images. In the case of either medium a large collection of hues and tones facilitates the execution of an idea, helping to solve problems of composition, color, and expressive intent.

The number of prints and solid colors being produced continues to expand year after year. Colorfastness and dimensional stability have improved, although protection from ultraviolet (UV) radiation is still necessary. Even the best fabrics are not guaranteed to be permanently colorfast, but now UV-proof glass, UV-proof films that can be applied to windows, and lamps with very low UV emissions are available to protect and prolong the life of textiles.

Collecting Fabrics

The ideal situation for a quilter would be to have an enormous collection of fabrics ready at hand whenever inspiration strikes. Few of us can hope for such luxury. However, most quilters strive to develop some inventory of scraps from previous work, remnants, hand-me-downs, pieces traded with friends, and fat $1/4$-yard cuts (which measure 18 by 22 inches) or $1/2$-yard or yard lengths of the latest designs. As your passion for quilting grows, so will your collection.

A collection of fabrics not only gives you a ready source for planning a composition, but over the years it compensates for the fact that manufacturers and retailers do not offer every color or print style every year. If you buy only what you need for a particular quilt at one time, you may find that it's no longer available should you decide to buy more for the border or the binding. If you don't have enough of a particular fabric, don't despair. Look at this as an opportunity to find an interesting solution to the problem and to enhance the diversity of the completed work.

Estimating Yardage

How much fabric should you buy? As far as your collection is concerned that depends on your pocketbook and your storage capacity. For a traditional geometric or appliquéd quilt, you can cut paper pieces from the templates, set all the pieces for one fabric side by side, measure the area they cover, and multiply by the number of squares you need for your quilt. For a Log Cabin design, you can estimate your fabric requirements by the method described on page 44. For contemporary art quilts, spread out all your tracing paper pattern pieces for one fabric together, then

---

ADAPTING A PROJECT'S DIMENSIONS

The size of a bed quilt depends not only on the size of the bed but also on whether you want to have some tuck-in under the pillow, how far you want it to hang over the sides of the bed, and whether there are bed posts requiring a cut-out corner on each side at the foot of the bed. Flat sheet dimensions are a good starting point. The following is a list of these with corresponding measurements for suggested scale drawing sizes. Note that all measurements are in inches.

	Flat Sheet Sizes	Convenient Scale Size
Crib	32 × 41	8 × 10$1/4$
Twin	70 × 105	14 × 21
Double	80 × 105	16 × 21
Queen	90 × 110	18 × 22
King	110 × 110	22 × 22

Pillows can be any size or shape. Standard pillow forms, including rounds, are generally available in progressive 2-inch increments, from 10 to 20 inches. Cylindrical shapes are less commonly available. Placemats vary in size and shape, but 12 by 18 inches is adequate. The dimensions of wall hangings and other original quilting projects are limited only by your imagination.

measure the area covered. In any case, if you err on the side of buying too much you will have some left over for your collection. Beg small scraps from your friends or trade with them to increase the variety. Don't worry about buying 1/8 yard and having most of it left over. Those remnants will become the basis of your collection for future quilts. Buy larger pieces if you can afford it. Watch for sales at fabric stores, salvage good pieces from discarded clothing, and scout the yard sales and rummage sales.

I am fortunate to live only a half-hour's drive from one of the best fabric stores in the United States, G Street Fabrics, on the outskirts of Washington, D.C. In their quilting department they have a basket of small scraps priced at five cents each and a bin of 1/2-yard remnants. At every opportunity I look through that basket and bin for additions to my collection. The queen-size bed quilt "The Pedricks at Home" (see page 121) incorporates pieces of forty-nine nickel patches.

I have always used all-cotton fabric, which has excellent dimensional stability, is washable, resists *bearding* (the tendency of the batting's fibers to migrate through the pores of the fabric and appear as white hairs on the surface of the quilt), and is easy to quilt. If you are more daring you can try anything that falls under the heading of textile, as well as some items that don't, such as leather. Be aware, however, that you may be creating something that is not washable, and remember that heavy fabrics make heavy quilt tops.

Preparing Fabrics for Projects

Before you can cut your first shape, you must prepare your fabrics by preshrinking and testing them for colorfastness. Get into the habit of doing this to all your fabrics as soon as you buy them, so you can be sure that they won't shrink or bleed the first time you wash your quilt. This process also softens the fabric, making it easier to quilt and more pleasant to the hand.

Sort your fabrics by color. Be sure to unfold them first, or you may be left with a line where the fabric was folded on the bolt. This is particularly apt to happen with dark colors if the dye runs into the crease. Rinse all of one color together in cool water, either in the washing machine or in a sink. It's not necessary to use soap or detergent for preshrinking, but if you would like to remove the chemicals with which some fabrics are treated, add a detergent with a low pH. The resins that coat new fabrics can cause problems with some sewing machine needles; these are removed by rinsing alone. After rinsing, spread the fabrics out to dry or tumble dry on the low setting in a dryer.

As red fabrics tend to bleed, be sure to rinse them separately, checking to see whether the rinse water turns pink. If it does, pin a scrap of white fabric to the red cloth, rinse it three more times in salt water (1/2 cup of salt to 1 gallon of water), drying the fabric between each rinse and using fresh salt water and a clean white scrap each time. Another option is to add 1 1/4 cups of vinegar and soak the fabric overnight. In any case, the white scrap should not take on any of the red color during the last rinse in clear water.

After your fabrics have dried, straighten the grain while pressing each piece. The straight grain runs the length of the fabric; its threads are called the *warp*. At right angles to that, the cross-grain runs across the fabric from selvedge to selvedge; its threads are called the *woof* or the *weft*. The straight and cross-grains are stable; the *diagonal*, or *bias*, stretches.

A good cotton fabric can be torn in a perfectly straight line lengthwise (as in removing a selvedge) or crosswise to cut a length. The selvedge should be removed because it shrinks at a different rate from the body of the cloth and is usually stiffer. Some fabrics will spread along the torn edge making a narrow margin of loose weave not suitable for seam allowance. This can be trimmed off with a rotary cutter. An alternative to tearing fabrics is to pull a warp or woof thread and cut along the line made by the pulled thread. If the thread breaks, cut what you've pulled out, then fish for the end, pull again, and continue all the way across.

If you pull a fabric on the bias you will cause it to change its shape. Sometimes a fabric rolled on a bolt will have acquired a bias stretch. You can easily return the grain of a fabric to its original square state by pressing it while damp and pulling it in the opposite direction. It's very important to cut your pieces with the grain so they won't pull bias in handling.

BATTING

Batting is the layer between the quilt top and the backing. In addition to providing warmth, its bulk gives contour to the surface of the quilt when indented with quilting stitches. Batting, top, and backing layered together are referred to as the *sandwich*. Polyester batting tends to beard, which looks particularly unsightly on dark colors. Cotton batting and cotton-polyester blends beard less. You can use all-wool batting, which feels warm and soft but is not washable. Cottons should not be dry cleaned, so a cotton quilt filled with wool batting puts you in an impossible situation as far as laundering is concerned. For a thin or small quilt, such as the One-Patch lap robe in Chapter 3 and the Log Cabin coverlet in Chapter 4, plain white cotton flannel provides an alternative that is easy to quilt and not too bulky.

BINDING

The material used to cover the raw edges of the sandwich is called the *binding*. It can be made with fabric cut either on the straight of the goods or on the bias. Bias binding is also available in the notions departments of fabric stores. The fabric of commercial bias bindings is not of good enough quality for a large quilt, but would do for a doll's quilt or other small project. The directions for binding each quilt are given with its general instructions.

Creating a Workspace

When you succumb to the enchantment of the art and craft of quilting, you will surely want to pursue further possibilities. A well-organized workspace will enable you to seek those goals more effectively. If you're fortunate enough to have a room of your own, maximize the light by painting the walls white or as close to white as possible. You'll need a large flat surface for cutting, either a table, a desk, or a drop leaf fastened to a wall. A separate table for your sewing machine would be a welcome luxury. You'll also need an auxiliary light for close work.

If you can spare the space, cover a wall with white felt, interfacing, cork, or some kind of wall board that will accept push pins. You can then use this surface to pin up your traditional quilt squares to decide on their sequence. Felt or interfacing will usually hold the work without pins, making it easier to rearrange the pieces. I use machine-washable acrylic felt. When you are ready to design an original quilt, such a wall will help in developing your plan. Creating in any medium, including fabric, can be done more successfully if you can assess your work from a distance frequently. Stepping back shifts

your focus from concentrating on the small details to evaluating the impact of the composition as a whole.

You can get an even better perspective by looking at your design in a mirror hung on the opposite wall, or, if you can't spare the wall space, on the back of a door. A mirror also reflects light, increasing the general illumination of your workroom.

Keep in mind that the floor of your studio will inevitably be littered with bits of thread, shreds of fabric, and pins. Unless you enjoy running the vacuum cleaner while crawling on the floor, upholstery attachment gripped firmly to resist the coiling hose, a shag carpet is not suitable. I prefer a vinyl floor that I can sweep and swab quickly. If carpeting is important to you, then the flatter the weave the better.

ORGANIZING AND PROTECTING YOUR FABRICS

In order to get the most out of your fabrics, you should invest some time and effort in organizing a storage system. In my studio I use an old chest, each drawer of which contains several sheets of corrugated cardboard. These serve as trays for various classifications

of fabric. The reds are all in one drawer, dark prints on one tray, bright prints on another, and solids on a third. I use four narrow drawers for trays of small scraps that I've sorted by color. When the chest is full I revise the system. You could use shelves, but the fabrics should be protected from ultraviolet light in some way.

While making "The Flaming Chalice" quilt shown in Chapter 9, I first pinned its cut shapes on the wall, then whole sections as I completed the piecing process, which took about two months. When I was nearly finished I realized to my horror that the blue border fabric had faded along the upper right corner. My studio faces north and is partly below grade, which allows for minimal exterior light, but as a precaution I always keep the curtains closed. Unfortunately, I did not consider the possible effects of the florescent lights, which were very close to the quilt's border. As a result, I was forced to remove that fabric and replace it with another manufacturer's dark blue. Now I am more conscientious about storing fabrics in drawers, and I hang a sheet over work pinned on the wall or on the quilting frame whenever I'm not working on it.

(Left) Fabric can be secured to a white felt wall either by friction or with pins.

(Below) I've organized my fabric collection in an old storage chest. The larger drawers each hold one color, while the small drawers contain a variety of small patches and scraps.

(Opposite page) My drawing table, here shown with an assortment of templates: balloons cut from old file folders; small triangles and squares of clear plastic with seam allowances marked with white peel-off paper; larger squares, a star, and a flower, all in translucent plastic; a clear plastic paisley stencil; and a rope border template cut from white card stock.

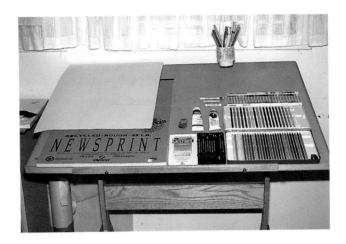

CHAPTER 2

QUILTING, COLOR, AND DESIGN

 ven though as a quilter you won't be mixing colors as a painter does, an understanding of color and design is fundamental to the success of your projects, whether they be traditional patterns or original designs. ❧ You need to discover your personal response to color while educating yourself about the objective rules of color relationships. The choices that result in compelling and appealing color schemes are based on both subjective and objective criteria, and your projects will reflect your ability to make balanced, informed, and creative decisions.

(Opposite) WOODLAND CREATURES *by Sarah Crooke. 1972. 81 × 93 inches.*
This quilt is an example of a prestamped design stitched with fine hand quilting.
Notice how carefully the quilting pattern fits each space. Photo by Breger and Assoc., Inc.
(Above) My drawing table, shown here with an assortment of sketching tools and materials:
sketching paper, drawing pencils, colored and charcoal pencils, pastels, and acrylic paints.

Developing a Color Awareness

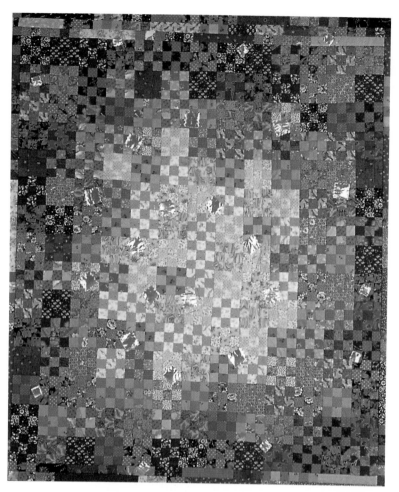

How do you become conscious of your color identity? Start by looking around you, noticing which hues and combinations you prefer. Visit a fabric shop and pick a dozen bolts off the shelves that catch your eye at first glance. Stack them together and look at them from a distance. Is the general impression a close harmony of a few hues? Is each of these represented in a range from dark to light? Are they pure and clear, or deep and subtle? Does one color predominate? Do the darks outnumber the lights, or vice versa? What combinations cheer you and make you feel comfortable? If you could choose the hues of the spaces in which you live and work, what would they be?

Go to a museum or gallery or browse through a book store or the art section of your public library to look carefully at great paintings. When a work of art has a strong positive emotional impact on you, notice the mood of the piece, which hues are included, and how they relate to each other. If you repeat this exercise several times you'll find that you respond consistently to certain palettes and arrangements. This will reveal your natural affinity for specific chromatic relationships.

Some quilters prefer strong contrasts of intense color, such as those that can be seen in the work of Dorothy Holden (see pages 6 and 122) and Kai Rim Park (page 11), while others favor somber tones. Some have favorite hues that consistently dominate their work, and others like a wide range of pale tones, which Christine Adams used in "There's No Place Like Home" (below left). Any of these combinations can provide the means to produce outstanding work. If you enjoy deep, rich hues, you'll do best designing with those. If you're happier with soft pale tones, they'll give you greater success. If your temperament is expressed by vivid colors, your work will be stronger if you follow that inclination. You will attain your greatest potential if you discover your own style and express your ideas through that. Regardless of the palette you favor, its use will be strengthened as you learn about color relationships.

Understanding color terminology and expanding your knowledge about color theory are essential in making color work for you. When you look at a painting or a quilt, make note of which part of the composition catches your eye first, then try to be aware of the path your eye follows in scanning the rest. By manipulating color relationships, you can also lead a viewer's eye through the design of a quilt on precisely the path you set.

(Above)
WHIRLPOOL
NEBULA.
*Photo by Mark
Gulezian.*

(Right)
THERE'S NO
PLACE LIKE HOME.
*Photo by Breger
and Assoc., Inc.*

*Two quilts by
Christine Adams
whose designs are
based on a range
of pale tones.*

Color Relationships

We see every color in relation to others. We call these relationships *contrasts*. These contrasts can be defined in terms of the following color characteristics:

- *Hue*, such as red, blue, yellow, green, and so on
- *Value*, a color's relative lightness or darkness
- *Intensity* or *saturation*, a color's degree of purity
- *Temperature*, a color's relative warmth or coolness
- *Extent*, which refers to the size of the area covered by a hue
- *Complementarity*, which indicates that two colors are opposite one another on the color wheel (see "Hue," below)

HUE

If you project a beam of light through a prism, the light will be refracted into the colors of the spectrum. The three *primary colors* are red, blue, and yellow. These provide the most vivid contrast because no other colors can be mixed together to produce them. By arranging them in a circle and mixing each of two adjacent primaries, you can create the three *secondary colors:* violet (red + blue), orange (red + yellow), and green (yellow + blue). The secondary colors are less intense because they are mixtures. Each secondary color is the complement of the primary color directly opposite it on the color wheel. Between the primary and secondary colors are *tertiary colors,* each of which is a mixture of its two adjacent neighbors; for example, yellow + orange = yellow-orange, blue + green = blue-green, and so on. You could go on mixing an infinite number of gradations, but the first twelve will serve the purpose of our discussion.

VALUE

As stated above, a color's value is its relative lightness or darkness, the result of mixing a pure hue with white (producing a *tint,* a lighter color), black (creating a *shade,* a darker color), or gray (resulting in a *tone).* The designs of many fabrics depend entirely upon contrasting values.

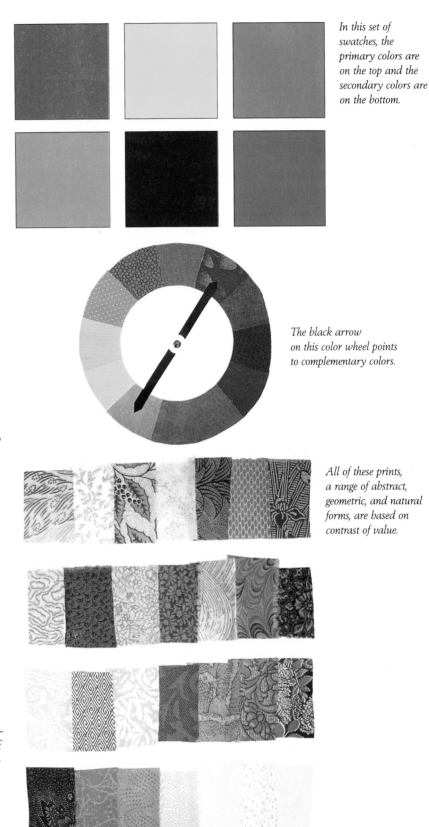

In this set of swatches, the primary colors are on the top and the secondary colors are on the bottom.

The black arrow on this color wheel points to complementary colors.

All of these prints, a range of abstract, geometric, and natural forms, are based on contrast of value.

INTENSITY OR SATURATION

A hue is at its most saturated if it is absolutely pure; that is, if it is undiluted by either its complementary color, black, or white. As a pure hue is mixed with another hue or with black or white, it becomes increasingly dull. A color of medium intensity that is placed next to its pure version appears duller than when it is next to a hue of low intensity. Color schemes consisting of low- and medium-intensity colors generally have a soothing effect on the eye because the contrast between them is limited. A small spot of high intensity can also attract attention to other less saturated passages of that same hue. This is just one of the ways in which you can direct the path of the viewer's eye in your quilt designs.

TEMPERATURE

The extremes of color temperature are red-orange, which is the hottest, and blue-green, which is the coolest. Whether a color gives the impression of being cold or hot depends on its surroundings. For example, if you place a color of medium temperature next to red-orange, the former will seem cool. If you then place it next to blue-green, it will appear warm. Temperature is a very powerful property of color. Have you ever noticed that you feel and look warmer in a red sweatsuit than you do in a pale blue one?

EXTENT

If one hue in a design covers a much larger area than any others, the design will take on the expressive or emotional tone of that hue.

When planning your designs, remember that *color is a builder of space.* In other words, certain colors within a composition will appear to advance or move toward the viewer, while others will seem to recede or move back into the picture plane. In general, red, light, brilliant, and warm colors advance, while blue, dark, dull, and cool colors recede. Remember that we see every color in relation to (by contrast with) others. If you choose primary red as the dominant color of your quilt, it will command attention as the most potent hue. On the other hand, even a large area of primary blue will recede when a small spot of orange appears within it. Pure yellow will shine brightly against any deeper color, but fades against a pale one. Note, however,

A color of medium intensity appears dull when compared to its pure hue.

The same patch of medium intensity next to one of low intensity seems brighter.

A swatch of medium temperature next to red-orange seems cool.

The same swatch next to blue-green seems warm.

If you stare at this red spot for a minute and then glance at the white of the page, you will see its gray-green afterimage.

that these tendencies are all modified by each other; that is, a dull, cool red will not necessarily advance when next to a warm, brilliant blue.

COMPLEMENTARY CONTRAST

Once I was at a concert watching intently as a performer played the piano. After a while I glanced at a large yellow moon projected on the backdrop. There, clearly defined, was a dark shape that I realized was the performer's head and his microphone. This strange image was not a shadow, but an optical illusion known as *afterimage.* If you stare at the red swatch at right and then look at the white of the page, you will see a greenish-gray square. Your eye has been fatigued by too much of one color and seeks relief by finding or creating its complement, the part of the spectrum that is absent from the color you've been focusing on.

Your eye is attracted to the area of a composition that contains the complement of its predominant color. If that is not supplied, your eye will generate the illusion of it. The tension between the physical needs of your eye and what is actually there creates a vibrancy that makes the work more exciting. This phenomenon can determine the path by which the viewer surveys your image.

Use the color wheel on the previous page to determine the complement of the color of any fabric. A straight line bisecting the color wheel will always indicate complementary colors. When you place complementary colors side by side, each intensifies the other. The traditional red and green of Christmas and the yellow and violet of Easter and spring are both good examples.

Choosing a Color Scheme

Color schemes are chromatic relationships on which to base your fabric choices. Using a color wheel as a guide, you can choose sets of hues that include the entire spectrum—dyads, triads, and tetrads—or others, such as analogous or monochromatic schemes, which use only part of the spectrum.

DYADS

Dyads are pairs of complementary colors. As explained above, these pairs include one primary and one secondary, which is composed of the other two primaries, thus including the whole spectrum. For example, the complementary colors blue and orange consist of blue and—within the orange—yellow and red. Complementary pairs are both harmonious and vivid in contrast.

TRIADS

A *triad* is one type of three-color scheme. If you rotate an equilateral triangle on a color wheel, it will always point to three equally spaced hues. These will be either all three primary colors, all three secondary colors, or one of two sets of tertiary colors. An isosceles triangle, which has two sides of equal length, would point to different sets of triads. The two points at the base of an isosceles triangle would always bracket the complementary color of the hue at its apex. For example, if the apex of the isosceles triangle points to yellow, then the two lower angles would indicate blue-violet and red-violet, which occupy the spaces on either side of yellow's complement, violet.

TETRADS

The color wheel can also be divided into sets of two complementary pairs by rotating a square or a rectangle on it. These groups of four harmonious colors are called *tetrads*. By drawing lines on both diagonals through either of these figures, you'll connect two pairs of complementaries.

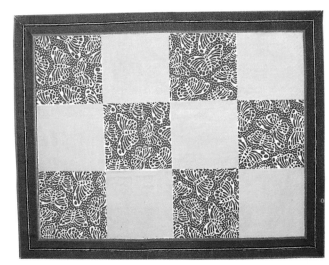

The complementary dyad of blue and orange is used in this straight-set checkerboard and repeated in the border.

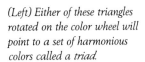

(Left) Either of these triangles rotated on the color wheel will point to a set of harmonious colors called a triad.

(Right) Either the square or the rectangle can be rotated to point to two pairs of complements that together make a harmonious group of colors called a tetrad.

We see every color in relation to others. These fabric squares show how different backgrounds affect each of the primary hues.

OTHER COLOR SCHEMES

You can plan color schemes that do not include the full spectrum by using an arc of the color wheel consisting of several adjacent hues. These are called *analogous color schemes.* One example would be yellow-orange, orange, red-orange, and red. *Monochromatic color schemes* are those in which several tints, shades, and tones of a single hue are used. Be aware, however, that a monochromatic design can easily become visually tedious. For instance, when designing the pink composition shown on the opposite page, I became so uncomfortable with all those rosy tones that I had to add a spot of turquoise for relief. Cover the turquoise spot and notice the difference. Your eye is still drawn to the woman's head first because it is attracted to the point where the lightest light (the highest value) meets the darkest dark (the lowest value). When you reveal the turquoise spot, notice how the womans' head as the central element of the design is strengthened even further. By adding contrast of hue to the area of the design where the strongest contrast in value occurs, you've captured the viewer's attention by accentuating the center of interest.

Another way to create harmonious color schemes is to combine colors of the same intensity or saturation. Compared with the vibrant free-form composition on the opposite page, its pale twin has an entirely different effect.

Reading about color theory will help you understand how and why certain color combinations and their arrangements in quilts and paintings affect you as a viewer. But the real learning takes place when you try out combinations yourself. Gradually you will assimilate the practical effects of combining fabrics. Making fabric studies like the ones that illustrate this chapter can provide a fascinating way to explore color and to develop designs at negligible cost. By cutting small pieces of fabric and pasting them on paper, you don't have to worry about sewing techniques. Instead, you're free to just relax and enjoy playing with color and shape.

These two studies, which use the same fabrics for an analogous color scheme—a tint of red, red-violet, violet, blue-violet, and blue—show the interplay of cool receding color and warm advancing color. The pink squares seem to hover in front of the blue-violet background while the blue ones float behind the surface, giving the composition a luminous and mysterious quality. This effect is cancelled out in the study with the pink background by covering part of the blue-violet fabric with red-violet and part of the blue with violet.

A single-hued image in a wide range of values is strengthened by the addition of a small area of contrasting hue.

(Below left) A composition of intense hues has a strong visual impact. (Below right) By lowering the intensity of some of the fabrics the effect of the image is transformed.

How Fabric Pattern Affects Quilt Design

When I first started quilting I collected pretty little floral prints and not much else. It wasn't until I ran across a notebook of fabrics that were classified under several categories, including hue, tint and shade, print scale, visual texture, and subject (such as florals, geometrics, stripes, dots, border prints, animals, people, architectural subjects, fruits, and foliage), that I realized how limited my selections had been and how boring the results. The four renditions of the traditional quilting pattern Variable Star, shown at right and on the opposite page, illustrate the importance of this point.

Be sure that your collection and your quilt designs include small-, medium-, and large-scale prints. However, bear in mind the scale of the project you're working on: A print that would be too large for a small pillow might seem small on a large bed quilt or wall hanging. When quilting a landscape, in addition to applying the adage "color is a builder of space" as a rule of thumb, use larger-scale prints in the foreground and choose progressively smaller ones as you select fabrics for images that gradually recede into the "distance." The subjects of the prints should also be appropriate to the image.

Prints with stark contrast, particularly those with pure white backgrounds and those with too many colors, are seldom suitable, although you will find some exceptions. In general, I buy very few high-contrast or busy prints unless they are unusually beautiful or suggest some special use, and I try to avoid small prints with more than two colors. Small prints can give the effect of solids from a distance, as can tone-on-tone prints in a single hue. Both are richer and more visually interesting than solid colors and can serve as textured backgrounds for the principal subject. Medium-sized prints offer variety of scale and can carry more hues successfully. Large-scale prints usually include, and can more easily accommodate, an even wider range of colors. Cutting small pieces from different areas of one large print can give the impression of a greater selection of harmonizing fabrics.

Stripes are useful as narrow outline strips or for borders to emphasize the framing of a scene or square. They can also make interesting sashes. Border prints, which incorporate two designs—one along the border, and one for the remainder of the fabric, which is called the *field*—can provide a wealth of options in a single color scheme, striped and otherwise. Solids can give your designs a bold,

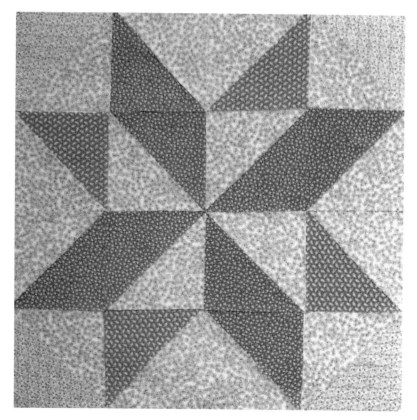

modern look, so if you prefer a softer or more traditional style, use them sparingly. In general, pale tints are more effective than pure white, and very dark shades of other hues are more intriguing than pure black. Some artists make it a policy never to include black in their palettes. You can even expand your field of expertise—as well as color choices for projects—by cultivating dyeing skills. Hand-dyed lengths of fabric are also sold through advertisements in quilting magazines and in some fabrics shops.

Texture can be created by using either pile fabrics, such as corduroy, velvet, satin, or velour, or by exploiting the optical illusion created by a printed design. It should be noted, however, that pile fabrics will shed along the cut edge and will slide around on the backing when you try to sew a seam. For these fabrics use a 1/2-inch seam allowance and pin and baste adequately.

Reflectivity is another characteristic that can add interest to a composition. Before you become charmed with its glamour and sparkle, note that lamé is not washable, so its use is generally confined to wall hangings that need only be vacuumed or that can be dry cleaned. Fusable webbing provides stability for lamé and, during piecing, it should be pressed with a cool iron and protected by a press cloth or it will melt. If lamé's limitations seem discouraging, there are many cotton prints with a metallic component that are washable. Some handsome examples can be found among upholstery fabrics. Their care instructions do not recommend washing, but I've washed some of these successfully. Iridescent fabrics made with one color in the warp and another in the weft shimmer and shine with changes in the light. When arranged in various directions, velvet, corduroy, and other piled and napped fabrics can look like different tones of the same fabric. For a matte finish there are flannels, ultrasuedes, and others.

Slipcover fabrics create possibilities for larger-scale designs and a greater range of more permanent colors. These are heavier than quilting cottons and, as a result, more difficult to quilt, but under special circumstances the extra trouble is worthwhile.

Each fabric should contribute to the goal of your design. If one print attracts attention to itself, remove it unless you deliberately want to make it a focus. For example, when selecting fabrics for the One-Patch quilt in Chapter 3, I ruled out many in my collection because their hues were too intense, their blues too green, or their pinks too orange. I decided instead to work with warm blues and cool pinks of moderate to low intensity. Yes, blues can be relatively warm if a little red is mixed in, and pinks can be cool if a little blue is present.

These four squares show the traditional quilt pattern Variable Stars in four different layouts: (Opposite, top) This square uses four small-scale prints without much light/dark contrast. (Opposite, bottom) This square shows four small-scale prints in a modest range of light, medium, and dark shades. (Top) This square uses four prints in a range of scale (small, medium, and large) and strong contrasts of light and dark and divides the large center square into four triangles. (Above) This square uses six prints in a range of scale and contrast and a border print in the center

Setting Traditional Squares

These squares are "hung on the diamond" or "on point." The color scheme—orange, green, and violet—is a triad.

This color scheme, a dyad of blue-green and orange plus neutral tones, was taken from the hues of the dominant print. The layout demonstrates the sequence of piecing for sashes, posts, and borders.

Patchwork squares can be sewn together, or *set,* in several ways. One treatment is to sew the pieces in horizontal or vertical rows, then to sew the rows to each other (as with the One-Patch in Chapter 3), which is called a *straight setting.* Your squares can also be arranged in a *diagonal setting,* in which the squares are set on their points and triangles of another fabric are used to fill out the edges of the quilt. Sometimes the triangles are omitted, leaving the edges zigzag. The squares in a diagonal setting are also called *on point* or *hung on the diamond.*

A collection of squares can be expanded by adding horizontal and vertical sashes and a border. The lap robe on page 96 is a good example of this kind of layout. A more elaborate arrangement adds posts where vertical and horizontal sashes intersect. These square posts, which are equal in width to the sashes, are sewn to the horizontal sashes to make a continuous strip of fabric sewn between larger rows that are composed of pieced squares and vertical sashes. Sashes and posts can also be added to a diagonal setting. The *streak of lightning* or *herringbone* setting, in which blocks set on point are sewn to triangles to make vertical rows, combines techniques from both straight and diagonal layouts.

Another way of expanding the area covered by your pieced squares is to alternate them with plain squares that are then made more interesting by the addition of quilted lines or patterns. The final effect is that of an eye-catching checkerboard of quilted solid and pieced squares.

When choosing fabrics for sashes, posts, and borders, you must bear in mind their relationship to the pieced or appliquéd squares in which you have invested so much time and loving care. The squares should be the focus of your quilt, not their frames. You might want to reread the section on "Color Relationships" (pages 25–26) to review the properties of color that will serve these purposes best.

The streak of yellow-green lightning is the complement of the red-violet border. The diamonds are composed of the complements yellow-orange and blue-violet, making this color scheme a tetrad.

Creating an Original Design

This tattered reversible quilted boat pennant carries the initials of its owner beside the coiled reptile for which Rattlesnake Island is named.

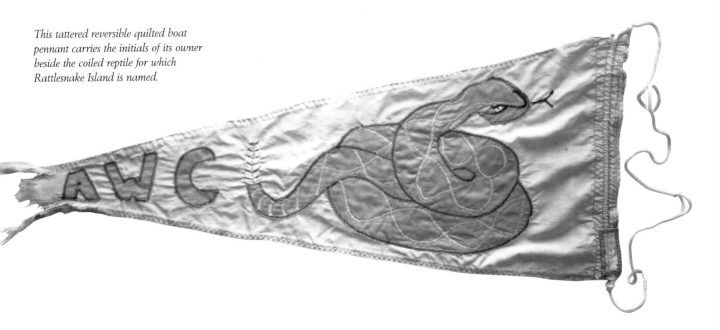

You want to create a quilt that is like a painting expressed in fabric, but how do you go about choosing a subject? An idea for a composition can come from anywhere and be as different in style as the impressionists are from the op artists. The idea for the well-worn quilted boat pennant above was taken from the name of the place where my brother spends his summers, Rattlesnake Island, New Hampshire. Years of windy trips across Lake Winnipesaukee have shredded and faded it, but it still snaps in the breeze over the bow.

A work of art points out and makes more evident the relationships among the various components of its subject. Forms of similar shape call attention to each other. The human and animal figures in "The Pedricks at Home" (see page 121) are an example of this. Similar values form patterns; similar hues echo each other. Our eyes make connections and track relationships, giving movement and energy to our experience of the work. In this way a composition can be very animated, much more than simply an accurate record of an object or a scene. An effective design is unified by rhythms of form and line. These effects are especially important in an abstract composition, where there

isn't necessarily a real object from which the image has been abstracted. In this way, we share the artist's feelings about the world.

When first you glance at a scene, you get a general impression: the major features, shapes, and colors, along with a few details. A second glance gives you a little more information, and serious study yields much more. An artist tries to record quickly and later maintain whatever it was that created excitement in the first glimpse. This catches the visual dynamics, the relationships, tensions, movements, and patterns. When you decide to design an art quilt, keep in mind what it was about your idea that first excited you. If you get bogged down, refer back to that excitement and think about how you can bring it back to life.

One way to start an original quilt design would be to select an object that has a simple form and repeat that shape in several variations, as I did with the crib quilt in Chapter 9 (see page 114). You could arrange a still life, copy the composition of a favorite painting, or look to a landscape for inspiration. Take plenty of time to let an idea evolve in your mind, then sketch it, revise it, set it aside to rethink it, then revise it

again. Work on it in any medium you're comfortable with, then make a fabric study, changing and modifying the idea continually. It will grow and improve with every revision, and you'll learn something from each stage that will help you with future designs.

If you're planning a quilt that includes a portrayal of real objects, you may want to look for detailed photographs of these, not for the sake of reproducing minute detail, but to become familiar with your subject so you can then abstract a simpler form.

A last word about working out your own designs: Don't feel obliged to maintain an equal balance of hue, value, intensity, color temperature, complementarity, or proportion in your work. It is the deliberate imbalance of these and other factors such as linear direction or texture that make a work of art emotionally expressive. Segments of a composition can be made to stand apart by manipulating these elements. In painting there is both transparent color and heavy impasto applied with a palette knife. In textile there is both surface texture and the illusion of texture created by print. Become aware of what is most exciting to you in your own work, then build on that awareness.

A Third Dimension: Quilting Design

Holding the sandwich together is only one of the purposes of quilting. Also important are the linear designs that are superimposed on the pieced surface and the three-dimensional effect of the quilting stitches.

Hand quilting is usually done with a common in-and-out running stitch. The trick is to make the stitches, as well as the spaces between them, small enough to delineate a design clearly. Producing stitches of equal length, however, is more important than making them exceedingly tiny. This is accomplished more easily by bending the fabric up and down to load the needle than by stretching the fabric taut and tilting the needle up and down. Sometimes, particularly in England, a backstitch is used. In the middle band of the border of the Bargello lap robe (see page 63), I used a chain stitch to quilt, and the words of a sonnet as quilting pattern.

Machine quilting saves time. It's not meant to look like handquilting but it is handsome in its own way. Use a roller foot attachment as described in Chapter 1. If your machine does only straight stitching, use simple quilting patterns and strive for steady, even lines. Refer to the Bibliography for suggested reading on the subject of machine quilting.

The amount of quilting required depends in part upon the type of batting used. All-cotton batting must be closely quilted in lines $1/4$ inch to 2 inches apart. A cotton-polyester blend will be stable with quilting 2 to 3 inches apart. I use all-polyester because the lines can be as much as 4 inches apart, which allows for more creative latitude.

Whether stitched by hand or machine, the number of possible quilting designs and the ways in which they can be made to interact with piecing and backing are essentially limitless. The quilting pattern for the doll's Log Cabin coverlet (page 49) is called *stitch-in-the-ditch,* in which the quilting stitches fall into the little valleys formed by the seam lines. The Medallion shoeshine stool (page 68) is an example of *outline stitching,* which is done within the seam lines of the patches, in this case $1/8$ inch from the seam (although $1/4$ inch is customary). Your quilting design can also depart from the pattern set by the pieced seam lines. For example, the Pineapple Square stool cover on page 53 is quilted in

The picture frame on this quilted pillow cover is one piece of fabric whose contours are created by the quilting stitches.

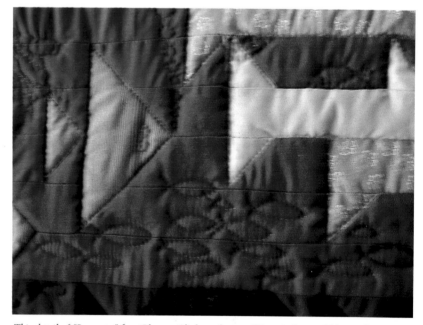

This detail of "Seascape" (see Chapter 9) shows how quilting stitches could be used to underscore a theme.

The presser foot has been removed, the tension loosened slightly, and a section of the sandwich clipped into an upside-down embroidery frame.

a circular pattern that cuts across seam lines but accentuates the piecing. "Seascape" and "Constellations" of the memorial quilt triptych (pages 124 and 125) are two examples of *echo-quilting*, in which the quilting lines emphasize the form of a motif. Some of the handstitching in "Seascape" also delineates underwater creatures, reinforcing the theme of the pieced image. The *grid-quilting* in the appliquéd Indonesian footstool (see page 78) flattens the background behind the initials, making them even more prominent.

An example of free-motion machine quilting is shown below. Free-motion machine quilting can be used to draw pictures, to write text, to embroider patterns, or to fill background areas with random stitching. The trick with this technique is to press the sandwich down onto the face plate near the needle with your fingers as you sew. Be sure to keep the presser bar lever down. I find myself automatically (and unnecessarily) raising the lever whenever I change direction, and because there is no presser foot I forget to put the lever down again, which leaves no tension at all on the top thread.

Scale is important, too, and should be related to the size and shape of the areas covered. Both density and scale are well planned in the embroidered quilt by Sarah Crooke (see page 22).

The completed pillow cover shows how free-motion machine quilting enhances the print design of the fabric.

CHAPTER 3

THE ONE-PATCH QUILT

he simplest patchwork pattern is composed of a series of rows of squares. If you've never attempted sewing of any kind, the One-Patch offers the opportunity to learn to use a sewing machine or to hand sew a straight line. You'll gain experience in fabric selection, preparation, and accurate cutting. You can also learn a trick or two for sewing the pieces together efficiently. Even with a simple One-Patch certain principles of color, scale, and design come into play. ❧ You'll gain an appreciation of the importance of accuracy at every step. When you make a mistake, as we all do, it won't cost you much time, effort, or expense to correct because the project, a doll's lap robe, is so small. And, because of its size, it will take far less time to complete than a full-size quilt. You'll experience the satisfaction of accomplishment that much sooner.

(Opposite) The finished One-Patch quilt shows a pale binding around the darkest blue pieces effectively bracketing the heart. Photo by Breger and Assoc., Inc.
(Above) Kathryn was made by Sharon Provost and dressed by the author.

Project: A Doll's One-Patch Lap Robe

Kathryn, the doll for which this quilt was made, is 28 inches tall, so her lap robe will have a finished measurement of approximately 18 by 24 inches. If you don't have a doll, you could use your One-Patch as a table cover or wall hanging. If you would like to adapt your One-Patch to a larger size, refer to "Adapting a Project's Dimensions," page 18. Also consider how the issue of scale (see box below) would affect a larger One-Patch.

ESTIMATING YARDAGE

For a small quilt of such a simple design, estimating yardage is not a problem. A 1½-inch square is a good size for this project. Because you need a ¼-inch seam allowance on all sides, you should cut 2-inch squares. The quilt top will be twelve squares wide by sixteen squares long. If you use only two fabrics and make a checkerboard design, you only need ⅓ yard of each fabric (which would be 12 inches long by an average

45 inches wide) to cut all 192 squares, or 96 squares each, with some small scraps left over for your collection. For greater variety, buy the smallest amount you can of as many different fabrics as your budget will allow.

Theoretically, a ½ yard (18 by 45 inches) should be enough for the backing, but that's too skimpy an estimate. The fabric may shrink slightly and the patchwork top may turn out (as it did in this case) to be a bit larger than planned. So buy at least ⅝ yard of the backing fabric, whose colors should harmonize with the patches on the top. Since this is an old-fashioned quilt pattern, you may want to consider using unbleached muslin for a backing. Because the quilt is so small, a heavy white flannel will do as batting.

A commercial bias binding could serve to finish the edges. If you calculate the quilt's perimeter (24 inches × 2 + 18 inches × 2 = 48 + 36 inches = 7 feet), you can easily determine how much binding you'll need to buy or how much extra fabric to set aside. (Remember to add a little extra for overlap at the corners.) One package of ½-inch-wide double-fold bias binding in a coordinating color would be plenty. I found it convenient instead to use a straight strip of the backing fabric.

A spool of dual-purpose thread to match the backing will do for piecing and binding. I tied this lap robe instead of quilting it. For that purpose a hank of embroidery floss in one of the predominant colors is more than enough.

CUTTING THE FABRICS

You can determine the number of squares to cut from each fabric by counting the number of fabrics you have collected and then dividing that number into 192 (the total number of squares you need). However, it's not necessary to have an equal number of squares of each fabric. You might find some tiny scraps from which you could only cut one or two squares. Use them. They'll add to the charm of the finished work.

I decided to use two squares each of 96 different fabrics. (You could use four squares each of 48 fabrics or eight squares each of 24 fabrics, and so on.)

A MATTER OF SCALE

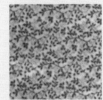

Before you search through a scrap bag or shop for fabric, consider the matter of scale. The design of the fabric print must be small and delicate for a work of this size. If you use a large flower print, only one or a few petals might show on a square. Even on a quilt of this size, however, you can provide variety of scale. The small prints should be the tiniest you can find and the larger ones would be considered rather small on a large quilt. To make the effect more attractive you'll need to provide variety in other ways as well. You could include flowers, stripes, dots, geometric or marbleized patterns, tiny animals, and other images. You might even try using the same print in different colors. Be sure these are distributed throughout the work, not placed side by side. For this quilt I even used the wrong side of one of the fabrics because I needed another pale pink and the right side was too intense.

The term "scale" also applies to the dimensions of the quilt's individual elements, which in this case are single patches. You wouldn't use 6-inch-square patches on this quilt. Such a design would require only three columns of four patches each. The quilt would be the correct size but it would be too coarse when draped over the doll's lap, and it wouldn't have enough variety of color and pattern. So the squares should be small. For this project a 1½-inch-square is a good choice. While 1-inch squares would be daintier, they are more difficult to handle. To allow for the standard ¼-inch seam allowance all around, cut 2-inch pieces for 1½-inch finished squares.

A small square cut from a large print (top) becomes an abstract form whose lack of identity may not suit your purpose. The rest of the designs—flowers, wildlife, dots, and lines—are within a range of scale that is well suited to small squares.

Cut 2-inch-wide strips long enough to yield the number of squares you need from each fabric—4-inch strips for two squares, 8-inch strips for four squares, 16-inch strips for eight squares, and so on. When all the strips are cut, lay each one along a vertical grid line on the cutting mat, and cut across the strip every 2 inches. When a print has a repeated image, try to place the ruler so that you can see a section of the design centered under it.

ORGANIZING YOUR CUT SHAPES

Even with a design as simple as this one there is ample room for creativity. Shown below are three of many possibilities. Play with various arrangements of these squares on a tabletop or a felt-covered wall (see Chapter 1). Shown below left is a pleasing random arrangement, an intuitive overall distribution of darks and lights, blues and pinks, with no discernable pattern. The effect is rather whimsical and quite lively, causing your eye to jump all over the surface.

The arrangement below, center, uses almost exactly the same set of patches but there is more of a sense of order. Your eye quickly finds a quiet path of moderate values running from upper left to lower right, which serves as a refuge from the far more active dark pink against light blue in the upper right and light pink against dark blue in the lower left. The entire layout is a

Hold the rotary cutter beside the metal edge of your transparent ruler, press down, and roll across the fabric.

checkerboard of two hues, but unlike a static checkerboard, there is movement, the result of changes in value. The pinks run from dark in the upper right to light in the lower left while the blues progress in the opposite direction. The dark blues are represented in greater number and therefore dominate. They are darker than the dark pinks so they anchor the composition. The contrast in the upper right is more luminous, almost as if a light were shining through from behind. Factors contributing to this effect include the small number of very pale blues, the purity of their hue, and the fact that the contrasting pinks are not only much darker, but also more grayed, less intensely pink, and

offer more variety of both shade and pattern. By comparison the pale pinks and dark blues occur in roughly equal numbers, and both are less grayed than the dark pinks. This layout could also be seen as a four-patch design, a collection of squares composed of two sets of diagonally opposite matched patches.

The layout I chose to use is shown below right. The squares are pinned to the felt wall in twelve columns of sixteen rows. I had to add one dark blue to the original collection and remove one pink in order to make the heart design. Here hue is the primary agent of design: the heart is one color and the background another. But value also plays an important part. The heart is darker around its perimeter and lighter in the center. It stands out against the background more clearly because the adjacent blues are pale. The darker blues form a frame for the composition. The effect here could have been more dramatic if I had made the patches smaller and increased the number of pale blues and dark pinks to delineate more clearly the perimeter of the heart.

PIECING AND PRESSING

The success of your quilt depends not only on your careful selection of colors and fabrics but also on the accuracy with which you put it together. On my sewing machine the edge of the presser foot is a hair over a 1/4 inch from the needle. Mark the needleplate of your

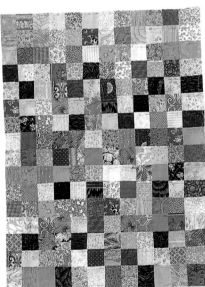

In this layout the patches are arranged at random. Contrasts between the lightest and darkest are scattered throughout, pulling your eyes here and there without coherent pattern. Photo by Breger and Assoc., Inc.

This arrangement of squares is a checkerboard of tonal gradations. Photo by Breger and Assoc., Inc.

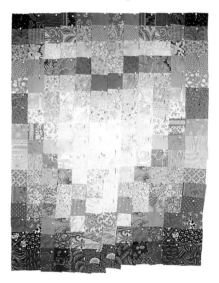

Here the layout is a pink heart against a blue ground. Set against the palest blues, the darkest pinks form the edge of the heart while the dark blues frame the overall composition.

machine a 1/4 inch from the needle with a piece of masking tape, but take up the tape and clean the plate after each project so that the mark will always be accurate. If it is off only 1/16 inch it will make a difference of almost 1 inch in the length and 3/4 inch in the width, which are big discrepancies for a little quilt.

Machine Piecing

1. Begin assembling your pieces by putting the first patches of columns 1 and 2 right sides together. Make sure that their corners are carefully aligned, and that their printed patterns are running in the right direction.

2. Pin the two squares together, then sew them exactly on the seam line, making two or three stitches on top of each other at the beginning and end of the seam.

3. Instead of cutting the thread at the end of the seam, put the second squares from columns 1 and 2 right sides together, then feed them through the machine after the first pair. Continue this procedure until you've finished sewing the vertical seams of the first two columns.

4. When you've finished columns 1 and 2, start again at the top of the quilt by sewing the first patch of column 3 to the first patch of column 2. Continue adding and stitching patches, column by column, until you've finished sewing the vertical seams of the entire quilt top.

5. An important part of the piecing process is the meticulous pressing of seams. As a general rule, you should always press seam allowances toward the *darker* of two fabrics to prevent their shadows or outlines from showing through. After you've pressed the vertical seams, you're ready to begin stitching your horizontal seams.

6. Fold the top row of patches down over the second row so that the right sides of the fabrics are together. Clip the threads between these rows so that you can see the vertical seam lines. Match these seams and pin through the seam allowance.

7. When every vertical seam is pinned in this row, sew the horizontal seam, then go on to the next row and repeat the procedure.

8. When you have sewn all the horizontal seams, check the right side of the quilt top before pressing. Make sure that all the squares meet precisely at their corners, all the seam lines are

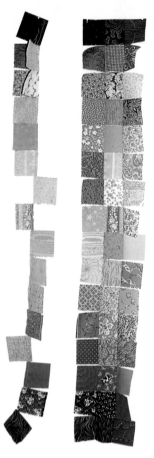 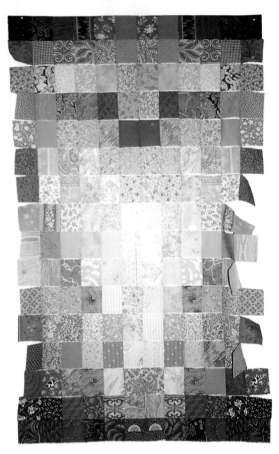

(Left) Sew the patches of the first two columns together in pairs, leaving the thread between pairs unclipped. (Center) Add patches, column by column, until you've finished sewing the vertical seams of the entire quilt top. In the photo at right, all the columns have been joined, but the horizontal seams are not yet sewn.

straight, the sides of the quilt top are parallel, and all the prints are right side up. If you find that some of the seams aren't sewn correctly, don't be discouraged. It's easy to rip them open and try again. The practice will pay off in the long run.

Hand Piecing

If you prefer to sew your quilt top by hand, you can follow a similar piecing strategy. Mark the 1/4-inch seam allowance on the top fabric of each pair of patches using a water-erasable fabric marker, pin them right sides together, and sew them exactly on the marked line. Do not sew into the seam allowance at each end. Leaving it free will make your job easier where corners meet. Since you won't be making chains of pairs as above, arrange your pairs in rows on a table or pin them to a wall to be sure they stay in the right order.

ASSEMBLING THE SANDWICH

1. Cut the backing and the batting an inch larger than the top.

2. Press the top, the backing, and the flannel batting, then layer them to create the sandwich. Pin the sandwich at the center, around the edges, and at several other points to keep the layers from slipping out of line.

TYING THE QUILT

When you use a batting that is unlikely to shift (such as the flannel used in this project), or when the batting is too thick for quilting, you can tie a square knot every few inches through all the layers of your quilt instead. Starting at the center of the quilt and working out to the edges, mark the top with a water-erasable pen or insert pins through the sandwich at regular intervals no more than 8 inches apart. These markings are usually made at seam intersections. Using a full six-strand embroidery floss, tie the quilt at every intersection, beginning at the center.

BINDING THE QUILT

1. Trim the edges of the sandwich so that all the layers are even. If you are

using bias binding, spread it open and place one edge against one length of the quilt top so that right sides are together. Pin them together at right angles to the edge of the quilt, then stitch them along the crease of the binding. Trim the ends of the binding so that they are even with the ends of the quilt. Repeat the procedure for the opposite side of the quilt.

2. Remove the pins, then turn the binding under so that it covers all raw edges. Make sure that the final fold of the binding lies along the seam line on the back of the quilt. Hand sew the binding to the backing.

3. After the long sides of the quilt are finished, place the binding along one end of the quilt top so that a 1/2 inch of binding protrudes at each corner. Pin and stitch the binding to the top as described in steps 1 and 2, then repeat at the opposite end. Fold the extra stub of binding around each corner to conceal all raw edges, then hand sew it in place.

I decided to use a remnant of the backing for this binding. I cut straight strips (not bias) 1 1/2 inches wide, folded

Layering a sandwich: Place the backing right side down, spread the batting over it, then lay the pieced top over that, right side up. Align all edges and corners.

them in half lengthwise right side out, matched the raw edges to the edge of the quilt top, and sewed along the seam line. I turned the folded edge to the back of the quilt and slip-stitched along the seam line, hiding the machine stitching beneath the binding. (*Slip-stitching,* also called *blind stitching,* is done by hand in such a way that the thread is hidden alternately under the quilt top or inside the binding so that only a tiny speck of thread is visible where it crosses between the two fabrics.) This provided a double layer of binding, with the corners finished as described above. See page 36 for the finished quilt, bound and tied. You can see by the stripes on the binding how each of the corners is finished with a butt joint.

If you've been making your own One-Patch as you read this chapter, all that remains is to embroider your name and the date on the back of your quilt. Congratulations!

Tying: Push the floss down through the sandwich, then bring it up again about 1/8 inch from where it was initially inserted. Add another stitch on top of the first. Pull the two ends snugly, tie them right over left, then left over right in a firm square knot.

Pin the folded binding to the sandwich so that raw edges are aligned.

CHAPTER 4

TRADITIONAL PIECING AND QUILTING

his chapter demonstrates the techniques involved in making two traditional quilting designs: the Log Cabin and the Pineapple Square. The Log Cabin is one of the easiest, most versatile, and most popular of the traditional quilting patterns. The earliest Log Cabin quilts of the 1860s were composed of strips of wool or silk fabric pieced onto a square cotton base. ❧ In contrast to the Log Cabin, which is today constructed by strip quilting without a fabric base, the Pineapple Square design is made by a method called *paper piecing,* which uses a temporary paper base on which the pattern is marked.

(Opposite) GREEN MANSIONS by Christine Adams. 1990. 54 × 54 inches.
While a quick glance at this quilt gives the impression of a traditional Log Cabin design, careful study reveals its complexity. (For a detail of one of the squares, see page 45.) Photo by Breger and Assoc., Inc.
(Above) A fabric study in progress for a large Pineapple Square project.

Project: A Doll's Log Cabin Coverlet

In order to demonstrate the principles involved in its design, the Log Cabin pattern as shown in this doll's quilt has been reduced to its simplest form. Once you understand the concept you can elaborate to your heart's content. The dimensions of the finished quilt are 14 by 17½ inches.

In the quilt I made for the demonstration, the center square, which is the darkest shade and the most intense hue, is surrounded by three pinks and three blues. Each of these hues is represented by two pale tones and one dark one. The print pattern in the center square shows a blue flower against a pink ground, incorporating both of the principle hues of the square. The other strips include a pale pink on white, a pale blue on white, two tiny floral prints, one stripe, and one marble print. These seven fabrics comprise the smallest number that could be used and still achieve the intended effect of the Log Cabin design.

ESTIMATING AND CUTTING THE FABRICS

To estimate the amount of fabric required, count the number of squares needed for the whole quilt (4 squares wide × 5 squares long = 20 squares). Each finished square is 4 inches on each side, including seam allowance. Then count the number of inches of each fabric in one square, including seam allowances. Since this is a very small quilt, I cut the strips only 1 inch wide to make ½-inch bands with a ¼-inch seam allowance on each side.

Center square = 1 inch per square
  (½ + ¼ + ¼)

First pink fabric = 2½ inches per square
  Strip One: 1 inch (½ + ¼ + ¼)
  Strip Two: 1½ inches (1 + ¼ + ¼)

First blue fabric = 4½ inches per square
  Strip Three: 2 inches (1½ + ¼ + ¼)
  Strip Four: 2½ inches (2 + ¼ + ¼)

Second pink fabric = 6½ inches per square
  Strip Five: 3 inches (2½ + ¼ + ¼)
  Strip Six: 3½ inches (3 + ¼ + ¼)

When you've counted all the fabrics, multiply the total length in inches of each fabric by 20 to find the amount needed for all the squares. To my total fabric count I added a border for the outer edge of the whole quilt, which I calculated to be 1½ inches wide (including seam allowances) by about 80 inches long (to allow for corners). The first pink fabric requires a 50-inch-long, 1-inch-wide strip, while the first blue fabric requires a 90-inch-long, 1-inch-wide strip. (This quilt doesn't require much yardage.) Cotton prints are usually made 45 inches wide. The 50-inch-long strip for the first pink fabric could be cut in two pieces and still require less than ⅛ yard, which is the minimum most fabric stores will sell.

Note that, in theory, the fabric I used for the center square should have required a 20-inch-long by 1-inch-wide strip, but because its blue flower motif repeats only every 2 inches I had to count out twenty blue flowers and cut the length necessary to include them all. I centered one flower in a square inch under my transparent ruler and cut each one separately. About half the fabric was wasted, but at such a small scale that didn't amount to much.

You could also use this method of estimating yardage if you wanted to adapt the Log Cabin design to make a king-size coverlet. On such a large quilt you would use wider strips, perhaps 2½ inches wide, and make your calculations in the same way. Once you know how to make your own calculations,

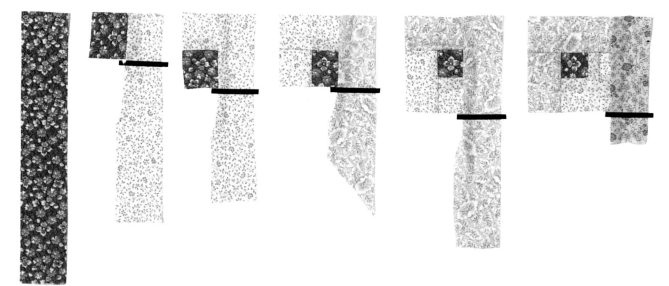

Note where the blue flower motif that I used in each center square repeats within the print. Because it occurs only every 2 inches, I had to count out the number of flowers I needed, not just the length of fabric required for that particular motif. A Log Cabin square is assembled by sewing strips of increasing length around a square center piece (continued on next page).

you won't have to rely on a book to list the yardage for exactly the size and style of quilt you want to make. For a larger quilt you would not only cut the strips wider, but you would also have more of them in each square. You would still include contrasts of hue, value, and type of print pattern, and the center piece would remain a focal point in some way.

Before cutting your fabrics, preshrink and press them as described in "Preparing Fabrics for Projects" (see page 19). As for the One-Patch quilt (Chapter 3), white cotton flannel is appropriate as batting for this small quilt.

PIECING AND PRESSING

As mentioned above, for the center square of this quilt I chose a fabric whose central floral motif measures less than 1/2 inch so that it could be seen within the square's perimeter. The central motif of the fabric you choose may be different, but make sure that you adjust your cutting and piecing so that the finished square makes the most of its design.

Ideally, your ironing board should be set up right at your elbow so that you can press every seam as you proceed. Because this doll's quilt is so small, a deviation of even one or two threads will appear crooked.

1. Carefully align the end of the first strip of the pink fabric on the center

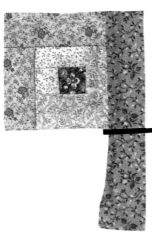

As you add each strip, trim off the excess to use for the next strip of that fabric. As shown on the back of the finished square, seam allowances are pressed away from the center with each addition. Photo by Breger and Assoc., Inc.

The Log Cabin squares in the layout at right are arranged to form chevrons, while in the one below they are turned to make diagonal stripes.

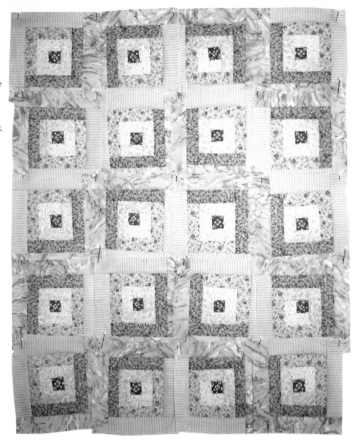

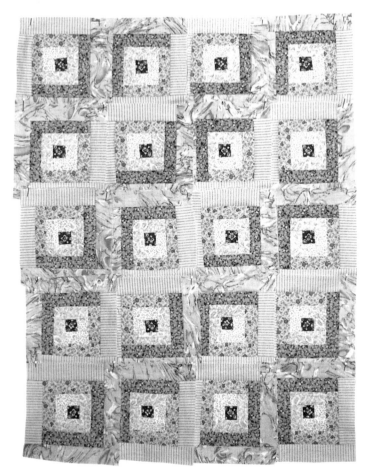

square, right sides together. Using a ¼-inch seam allowance, stitch the pieces along one side, trim off the excess from the strip, and press the seam away from the center. Although the center square is the darker of the two fabrics, press these seams away from it to avoid ending up with a thick lump of fabric in the center of each square.

2. Take your long strip of the first pink fabric and place the end of it on top of the first two pieces, right sides together. Stitch and press the seam, trim the excess fabric, and set it aside for the next square.

3. Set the end of your long strip of the first blue fabric face down on the right side of the growing square, then stitch, press, and trim the excess. Continue around the square, working clockwise, pressing and trimming each strip before adding the next. Remember to use each fabric twice.

SETTING AND ASSEMBLING THE SQUARES

Once you've completed piecing all twenty squares, experiment with a few arrangements by pinning them up on a wall or laying them out on a table. In addition to making those shown at left, I also tried looking at a layout in a hinged mirror. I decided on a popular setting that orients all the squares in the same direction (see page 49). After you've chosen a setting, you're ready to assemble your quilt top.

Using a ¼-inch seam allowance, sew the top square in column 1 to the top square in column 2. Follow the procedure for assembling the One-Patch quilt in Chapter 3 (see "Piecing and Pressing," pages 39–40). Connect all twenty squares, pressing each seam as you go.

ADDING A BORDER

If you would like to add a 1-inch-wide border like the one I added to the quilt I made for this demonstration, your fabric must be 1½ inches wide to accommodate seam allowances. To unify the design of my Log Cabin quilt I used the same fabric as for the center piece of each square.

Sew the fabric on in strips around your assembled squares. Each strip will butt up against the next, just as they did as you progressed around each single square.

By looking at a single square in a hinged mirror, you can evaluate a variety of settings.

(Below) A rolling presser foot allows machine quilting to proceed smoothly.

ASSEMBLING AND QUILTING THE SANDWICH

The backing I used is a solid color, one of the two hues of the quilt top. You can use either a thread that matches the backing or one that contrasts with it for the quilting stitches. I chose a paler pink. A blue would have brought the second quilt color onto the back of the quilt.

1. Cut the backing and batting an inch larger than the pieced top.

2. Press the top, the backing, and the batting, then layer them to create the sandwich. Pin the sandwich at the center, around the edges, and at several other points to keep the layers from slipping out of line.

3. Machine-quilt the sandwich using the "stitch-in-the-ditch" pattern. (The "ditches" are the little valleys between pieces and squares formed by the seam lines.) Sew the first quilting line down the center of the quilt, from the lower edge of the top border to the upper edge of the bottom border. Then sew quilt lines on the two other vertical seam lines between squares.

4. Starting with the center line, quilt the four horizontal seam lines between squares from border to border.

5. Run a quilting seam around the inner edge of the border, then on each square around the seam midway between the center and the edge of the square.

BINDING THE QUILT

The binding is a double one the same as that used for the One-Patch in Chapter 3. (See "Binding the Quilt," page 41).

The detail of Christine Adams's "Green Mansions" (see page 45) shows only one example of the infinite variety that can be explored within the Log Cabin format.

(Above) By looking at the back of the finished quilt it is easy to see how the quilting pattern is evenly distributed.

(Opposite) The top of the completed quilt shows still another possibility for arranging the same set of squares. Photos by Breger and Assoc., Inc.

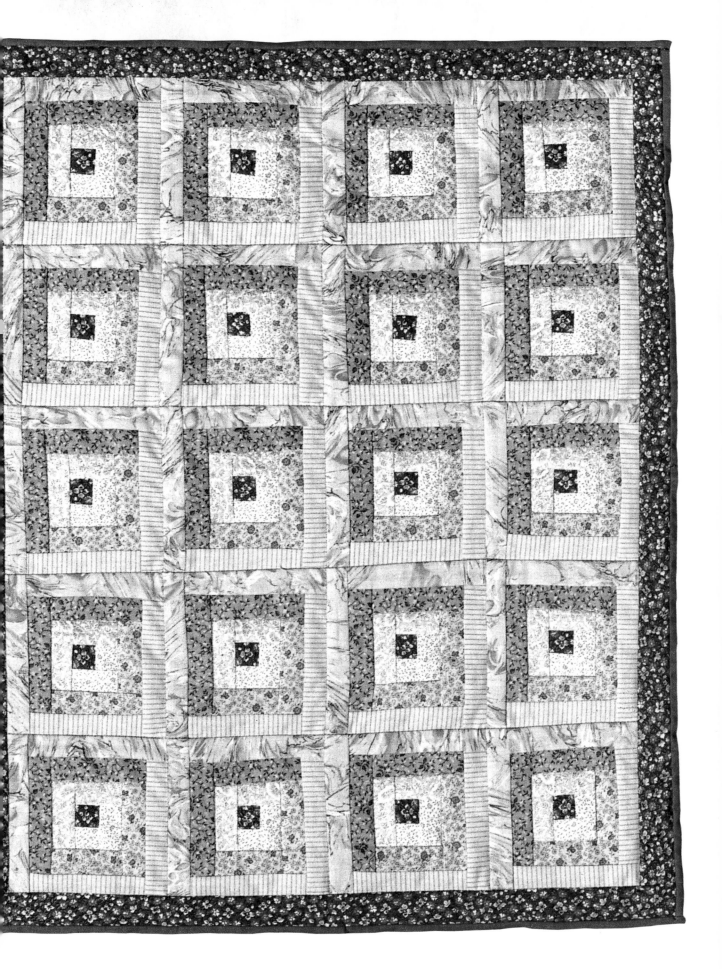

Project: A Pineapple Square Stool Cover

To make a Pineapple Square, strips of equal width are sewn onto the four sides of a center square piece, as in a standard Log Cabin. Because the Pineapple Square is an octagonal design, the assembled piece is then turned 45 degrees and the second rank of strips is sewn in the four diagonal directions. Another 45-degree turn puts the third rank of strips parallel to the first, and so on. It's easier to be accurate with this complex pattern when working on a paper diagram on which all the seam lines are marked. You could enlarge or reduce the pattern below on a photocopier for another project. To draw a paper pattern for this project, refer to the steps below, right. You can then photocopy your pattern to make as many squares as you need.

ESTIMATING YARDAGE

To estimate the yardage for this project, measure the top of your footstool. The footstool I used for this demonstration measures 11 by 14 inches. Rather than use one large Pineapple Square or a few medium-sized ones, I decided to divide the composition into four rows of five 3-inch squares, which allows for greater choice of layout. I then had to trim the squares along all four sides because the dimensions of the finished top were larger than the footstool's. I disguised this discrepancy by making all the border sides of the outer squares a single color framing the picture. If your footstool is a different size, make sure that the number of squares that you use covers the top completely. You can then trim off any excess.

The project shown is so small that only a small scrap of each fabric is needed. If you want to estimate yardage for a Pineapple Square of any size, draw your diagram in the size you need, then measure the total length of all the strips in the same fabric including 1/4-inch seam allowances. This is the length of the strip of that fabric you will need for one square. The width of the strip will be the width shown on your diagram, plus seam allowance. For example, in the 3-inch square used in the stool cover project, the strips are all 3/4-inch wide (1/4 inch for the strip + 1/4 inch seam allowance on each side). The length depends on how many strips of that fabric you want to use in that square. Multiply that sum by the number of squares in the quilt top. This

To draw a 3-inch Pineapple Square diagram for the fabric study and paper piecing steps of the stool cover project, refer to the example at left and follow these steps:

1. Draw a 3-inch square (the outermost red lines), then divide it in half vertically, horizontally, and on both diagonals (shown in green).

2. Draw a 1/2-inch square in the center, then add four more concentric squares at 1/4-inch increments (also in red).

3. Turn the diagram 45 degrees, draw a square (shown in blue) around the red center square so that each of the blue square's sides touch one of the four corners of the center square, then add four more concentric squares at 1/4-inch increments (also in blue).

4. Add a 1/4-inch seam allowance line around the outer edge of the largest red square (shown in brown). If you want to make a larger Pineapple Square, simply enlarge the dimensions. Remember when cutting strips for piecing to add a 1/4-inch seam allowance on each side.

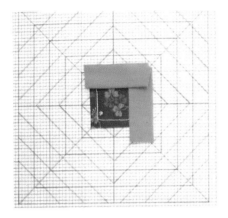

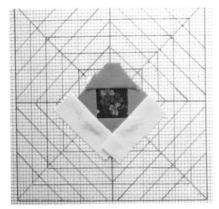

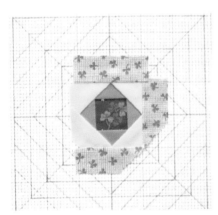

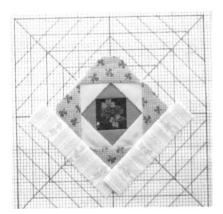

In a Pineapple Square, strips are sewn on four sides of the center square, which is turned 45 degrees before the next four strips are added.

OPTICAL EFFECTS OF INTENSITY AND VALUE

The entire color wheel is represented on the sparkling stool top, but the dominant contrasts are those of intensity and value. Look at the pot holder, which is a single pineapple square. Then look carefully at the single square on the paper pattern for the stool cover (see page 52). You will see that both squares are pieced on the same pattern. Now compare the pot holder to the finished stool cover (page 53). Both of these have strong contrast of hue, but that is not the critical factor. All the hues of the pot holder are intense or saturated colors. Its composition is bright, but not as exciting as that of the stool. In the stool cover pattern, the single square has been transformed within the context of the others by contrasts of both intensity and value. Instead of the Maltese cross of each single square you see four-pointed stars within circles. Now concentrate on the little dark blue squares in the stool top, and you will see pale pinwheels against darker color. Imagine that all the stars' intense hues were plain black. The pinwheels would then be the dominant image instead of the circles and stars.

This single Pineapple Square, which is bound as a pot holder, relies on contrast of hue for its impact.

51

When you cover all but one square of this quilt, the circles disappear and a Maltese cross is revealed.

gives you the total length of 3/4-inch strips that you need. Then divide that number by the width of the yard goods (about 45 inches) to find your required yardage, which may be only a few inches. You can see why the Pineapple Square is popular for scrap quilts. Nearly 900 pieces were used for the top of this stool.

MAKING A FABRIC STUDY

I started this project by doing a fabric study (see page 16) because I wanted to find out whether I had enough variety of dark fabrics of each hue to form the stars and enough variety of pale tints to compose the supporting arcs (see Color Note, page 51). Since no sewing is involved in a fabric study, you can cut the pieces without seam allowances. Usually a fabric study is done on a smaller scale, but because the stool top is so small it's easier to work at the same size.

SETTING THE SQUARES

I filled in all the spaces on my paper layout without regard to their relationship to each other (see photo, left). The composition looked unbalanced because the warm-colored stars were all on one side. I moved some of them to make the effect more comfortable.

CUTTING THE FABRICS

The smallest pieces of each square are isosceles triangles measuring a 1/2 inch at the base side and 5/16 inch on the two shorter sides. The tiny size of these pieces requires that their print patterns also be minute.

The largest pieces of each square are also isosceles triangles that measure 1 inch at the base and 11/16 inch on the shorter sides. These pieces gave me an opportunity to include some "surprises" in the design. In my collection of small scraps was a print of cats in various colors. It was possible by cutting carefully to show most of the nose, mouth, whiskers, and eyes of one cat in one of these triangles. I used these in the orange, red, blue, and turquoise sections of the work. You can't see them in the fabric study because I hadn't thought to include them at that point. Once it occurred to me, however, I began to look for other images that were small enough to fit these spaces. If you look carefully at the picture of the finished top at left, you will find a horse's head, a parrot, a deer, a woman paddling a canoe (the canoe isn't visible), and some lionesses.

After I finished the fabric study, I could see that the initial placement of the stars in orange, red, and pink—all hot colors—unbalanced the composition.

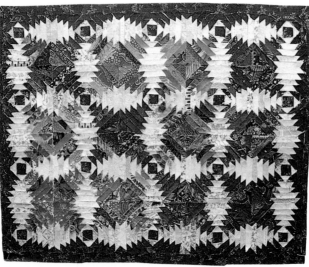

Moving the hottest color, red, to the right, helped balance the design. The completed quilt top sparkles with contrast of hue, tone, temperature, and intensity.

52

PAPER PIECING AND PRESSING

1. Set the first piece of fabric, a square, right side up on the paper. Then lay the second piece, a strip, on top of it, right side down, with the seam lines matched. Sew the seam right through the paper, then press open the second fabric to reveal its right side. Working around the original square, one rank at a time, turning the assembled piece 45 degrees for each new rank, add each piece of fabric in the same way.
2. As each rank is sewn in place and pressed, trim the ragged ends of the strips to reduce bulk.
3. Once all the rows of the paper pattern have been filled, peel the paper off the back.

To assemble the squares, see "Piecing and Pressing" in Chapter 3 (page 40).

ASSEMBLING THE SANDWICH

If you intend to use your pieced top as a stool cover, layer it with extra-thin batting and use muslin as a backing. Cut the batting and backing 1 inch larger than the top, then pin the sandwich to keep it from slipping. Since this quilt is too small for a quilting frame, you could use an embroidery hoop or you could quilt it without stretching it on anything. The quilting pattern is a series of overlapping circles that emphasize that aspect of the design.

If you prefer to adapt your Pineapple Square to some other purpose, follow the instructions for "Assembling and Quilting the Sandwich" for the Log Cabin quilt (see page 47).

FINISHING THE CUSHION

To make your own welt cord, refer to the steps above right. I sewed welt cord around the border (being careful to allow enough fullness at the corners), trimmed the seam allowance to a 1/4 inch, then added a band of plain blue for the sides, and quilted that also in overlapping circles to echo those on top. I chose not to use a second welt cord around the lower edge of the sides, although you may do so on your own cushion.

The top of this stool is a cushion mounted on a piece of plywood. I stretched the finished quilt top over it, folding the edges of the sides underneath and stapling them in place. I then put the cushion back on the frame and refastened it from below using four long screws.

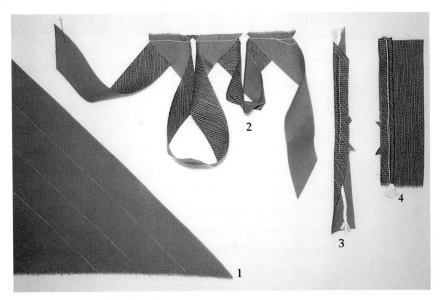

To make a self-covered welt cord:
1. Mark the back of the fabric with diagonal lines far enough apart to cover whatever size cord you are using plus a generous seam allowance.
2. Cut the strips and stitch them end to end.
3. Clip the threads that connect one seam to the next, finger-press the seams open, fold the strip around the cord, and stitch using a zipper foot.
4. Align the covered cord with the edge of the stool top, raw edges together, and stitch using a zipper foot.

The complexity of the finished stool invites close examination. I wasn't sure that anyone would notice the animal prints I had used in some of the squares, but when my five-year-old grandson, Billy, suddenly said, "I see your cats, Granny," as he ran his toy trucks over the quilting pattern, I knew I had accomplished my objective! Photo by Breger and Assoc., Inc.

CHAPTER 5

ADAPTING TRADITIONAL DESIGNS

The three quilting projects in this chapter use contrast of value as a major aspect of their designs. In order to portray a landscape seen through a window, "Billy's Window" adapts a traditional pattern composed of a square patch and two trapezoids that uses value contrasts to create an illusion of depth and distance. "Katie," a lap robe in a Bargello design, uses dramatic changes in value to create a feeling of rhythm and movement and to highlight border text. In the third project, a Medallion footstool, contrasting values are used to emphasize pattern in a flat plane.

(Opposite) CRAZY SUE IN THE ATTIC WINDOW by Dorothy Holden. 24 × 28 inches.
Collection of Merydyth Holmes. An unusual interpretation of the Attic Windows pattern,
this figure was assembled like a crazy quilt, then appliquéd onto the attic window. The orange floor and
cheerful backlighting create an inviting setting for a charming young lady. Photo by Joseph E. Garland.
(Above) This fabric study for a Mariner's Compass shows just one of many
possible variations on the traditional Medallion pattern.

Project: An Attic Windows Bed Quilt

After making a One-Patch quilt, a friend gave me some leftover scraps with fractions of images of animals, fish, racing cars, and other subjects of particular interest to boys. I looked through my books of traditional quilting patterns and found Attic Windows, a grid of windowpanes that presents an optical illusion of depth. The "glass" of the panes is usually shown in a solid dark color, as if there were no light on the other side of the window. The twin bed–sized quilt I made for this demonstration, "Billy's Window," is an adaptation of the traditional pattern, which solved the problem of how to use the fractured images. Broken up by the *mullions* (vertical dividers) and *muttons* (horizontal dividers) of the attic window, these images would appear to compose a landscape. In keeping with this idea, I quilted the border of the demonstration quilt in a pattern suggesting woodwork.

This scrap of fabric, which was left over from a friend's quilting project, poses a problem of how to deal with fragmented images.

DECIDING ON A COMPOSITION

What would you like the view from your window to be? Will it be one large, blossom-covered tree, a distant mountain, or a huge moose looking in at *you?* Or would you rather be on the outside looking in?

1. Make a rough sketch of your vision, simplifying the image as you work. Then enlarge your sketch to full size on sheets of newsprint that have been taped together. Simplify the image still further, making it similar to the kind of illustration used in books for toddlers. When it's complete, color it in roughly with crayons or paints.

2. Cut long 2-inch-wide strips of plain newsprint to use as mullions and muttons. Arrange them on top of your sketch to form a grid of 4-inch squares. Now you can see how many squares of each color fabric you will need. (Because this is only a paper study, the dimensions of its motifs do not include seam allowances.)

You are free to make the quilt any size, with any number and configuration of windowpanes. The information below on estimating yardage refers specifically to a twin bed–sized quilt measuring 70 by 88 inches, consisting of twelve rows of nine 4-inch squares, for a total of 108 squares.

ESTIMATING YARDAGE

Use the same method for estimating yardage outlined for the doll's Log Cabin coverlet in Chapter 4 (see "Estimating and Cutting the Fabrics," pages 44–45).

1. The mullions and muttons will be cut $2^1/2$ inches wide, which includes a $1/4$-inch seam allowance on each side. To calculate the number of inches of mullion strips you'll need, measure the length of a mullion on its longest side, add a $1/2$ inch for seam allowance (a $1/4$ inch on each end), and multiply by the total number of mullions in your quilt. Be generous and add a few feet to allow for miscuts and variations in fabric width. For the quilt I made for this demonstration, I calculated approximately 1,300 inches.

2. Divide the total number by 45 inches, which is the approximate width of the yard goods. You'll need about twen-ty-nine $2^1/2$-inch-wide strips, or about 73 inches of fabric, which equals a little over 2 yards. To allow for errors or shrinkage, buy $2^1/4$ yards of fabric. Use the same method to estimate the yardage for the muttons.

3. The windowpanes will be cut in $4^1/2$-inch squares, which includes a $1/4$-inch seam allowance on all sides. Refer to your full-size sketch to determine the number of squares you need in each color, then multiply by $4^1/2$ inches to determine the total length you'll need of each fabric. To calculate the yardage, divide each amount by 45 inches.

4. Because the finished border will be 6 inches wide, each long side requires a $6^1/2$-inch-wide by $72^1/2$-inch-long strip, and each short end requires a $6^1/2$-inch-wide by $54^1/2$-inch-long strip, all including seam allowance. It would be prudent to cut these four strips a couple of inches too long in case you didn't use the full seam allowance and the grid turned out larger than originally planned. You will also need four corner posts, each 6 $1/2$ inches square. If possible, use strips the same length as each side of the quilt so that you won't have extra seams along the border. If you buy $2^1/4$ yards you can cut four strips side by side: two strips $72^1/2$ inches long for the sides, and two strips $54^1/2$ inches long for the short ends. You'll have plenty left over for the four corner posts.

5. The backing is composed of three panels because the quilt is wider than a bolt of cotton fabric. Rather than make a seam down the middle, I centered a full-width panel in the same fabric as the border. This is flanked by two bands of bright red, a cheerful color for a boy's bed. Because the finished top including the border is 84 inches long and the backing should be cut 2 inches larger all around the quilt top, you'll need 88 inches, or a little over $2^1/2$ yards for the center panel, and another equal length that will be split down the middle for the two side panels.

6. The double binding, which matches the side panels of the back, is made from a 4-inch-wide strip that is twice the length (88 inches × 2) plus twice the width (70 inches × 2) plus a little extra for corners. A generous estimate would be 1 yard of fabric.

USING VALUE TO CREATE DEPTH

The grid dividing the panes of "Billy's Window" is in two tints of blue. While the contrast between these two tints gives the illusion of three dimensions, it also establishes the direction of a light source. Although blue generally recedes within a composition, in this case it advances because both tints are extremely light in value relative to the general tone of the landscape.

If you substitute tone-on-tone prints for the solid colors that are traditionally used in the Attic Window, the results will be more vibrant. Don't assume that you're limited to solid colors to express these effects.

In the Attic Windows pattern (left), value creates the optical illusion of three-dimensional form. The impression of texture, the direction of light, and the illusion of depth in the tree (right) also depend on changes in value.

CUTTING THE FABRICS

Cut 4½-inch squares and set them in the appropriate 4-inch square on your full-size sketch. The seam allowance will encroach on the paper mullion and mutton strips, but that doesn't matter. If you want to use a portion of a printed fabric so that it implies a continuous view over several panes, set the whole section on the sketch and mark where the muttons and mullions will cover the image. Add a ¼-inch seam allowance on all sides, then cut the fabric accordingly.

For example, I wanted to use a print of a seaplane where the sky and the land meet the water. I set it on my layout, marked where one mullion crossed it, cut out a vertical strip, trimmed the resulting two pieces to 4½-inch squares, and set them on two adjacent squares of my layout. Because the background on which the plane had been printed was white, I used thinned acrylic paint to color it to match the surrounding scene. (Note that acrylic paints will not wash out when laundered.)

For the demonstration quilt I didn't know exactly what features would be included in the landscape. All I had was a general idea that the scene would include a body of water, a village, land, animals, and sky. So, as I studied the scraps, I cut 4½-inch square images for the panes and arranged them on my felt design wall rather than on a full-size sketch. I placed the marine life with the darkest background at the bottom of the scene; above that, other underwater life printed against a lighter ground. At water level I added ducks, sailboats, and the seaplane. Next I worked on the banks of the body of water, which I filled with beds of flowers. Above them on the left I designed a forest with wild animals. On the right is a village with a school, a firehouse, a post office, a construction site, and even a racetrack. Balloons float in the sky on the left. Because I didn't have any prints depicting birds in flight, I painted a few patches of plain white cloth with thinned acrylic to create the panels I needed. This problem could also be solved by

appliquéing a shape over a background fabric, such as adding eyes, nose, and mouth over a textured brown print to create an animal's face.

The windowpanes are square, so the mullions and muttons are of equal length. The sum of the inner and outer long sides of a mullion or mutton is about 12 inches, including seam allowance. Cut the yards of blue strips into 1-foot lengths, then cut each of these in half at a 45-degree angle. This cutting method creates the mitered corners of the panes.

PIECING, PRESSING, AND ASSEMBLING THE SQUARES

Once you decide on the placement of your panels, you can begin piecing the squares. Each square is composed of three elements: a mullion, a mutton, and the square image in the pane.
1. Sew a mullion to a pane. Because the mullion is the lighter of the two fabrics, press the seam toward the pane.
2. Sew a mutton to the pane. Then press the second seam toward the pane.
3. Fold the square diagonally, then sew the mitered corner as an extension of the line of the fold. Press the seam toward the mutton, which is the darker of the two fabrics, then press the completed square.

When all the squares are sewn and pressed, follow the procedure used to assemble the One-Patch lab robe in Chapter 3 (see "Piecing and Pressing," pages 39–40).

ADDING THE BORDER AND ASSEMBLING THE BACKING

1. Cut the 6½-inch-wide border strips.
2. Pin the end of one of the border strips to the end of one side of the grid, right sides together.
3. Sew this seam and trim off the excess border. Do the same for the other three sides of the quilt.
4. Cut four 6½-inch corner border squares and sew them at the corners of the quilt.
5. Cut the center backing panel 4 inches longer than the length of the quilt. Trim off the selvedge Cut the two side panels so that when they are added to the center panel the total width of the back will be 2 inches wider on each side than the quilt top.
6. Cut the batting the same size as the backing. I used low-loft polyester batting on this quilt because a thicker or denser batting would be more appropriate for tying than for quilting.

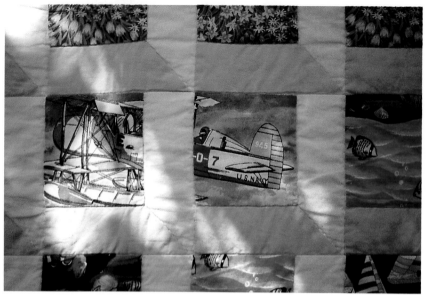

I cut the seaplane in half, trimmed it in the middle to account for the mullions and muttons of the window, and painted its background to match that of the adjacent squares.

Construct each square of the quilt top by assembling its three elements in the following sequence:
***1.** Mark a fabric strip to cut the mullions.*
***2.** Sew a mullion to a pane.*
***3.** Sew a mutton to the pane.*
***4.** To sew the mitered corner of the mutton and mullion, fold the square diagonally.*
***5.** A completed square with its seams pressed open.*

ASSEMBLING AND QUILTING THE SANDWICH

1. Press the top and the backing. Set the top aside.
2. Spread the backing right side down smoothly on a flat surface.
3. Spread the batting over the backing. Starting at the center and pressing out toward the edges, smooth out any wrinkles. Because batting is compressed to fit in the plastic bags in which it is sold, allow it to rest overnight so that it can resume its normal size.
4. Smooth both layers out and trim them so that they are at least 2 inches larger on all sides than the quilt top.
5. Lay the top on the batting and, starting at the center, smooth it over the batting. Pin it around the edges.

Machine Quilting

1. Using long glass-headed pins pointing in the direction of the seam, pin the length of the quilt in rows 6 inches apart, conforming to the window.
2. Roll the quilt parallel to the pin lines, both sides toward the middle.
3. Quilt the center first, removing pins as you go, and work your way out toward the sides.

Hand Quilting

To hand quilt a bed quilt of this size, you'll need a quilting frame. A quilting frame is composed of end pieces that are mounted on legs of some sort and bars that connect the ends to make a rectangular frame on which to pin the sandwich. One end of the sandwich is pinned to a strip of fabric stapled to the bar nearest the quilter. The bar is turned to roll the quilt like a window shade. The other end of the quilt is then pinned to a similar strip of fabric stapled to the other bar, and the quilt can be rolled back and forth between them as you quilt. Unless you first hold the sandwich together with large, loose hand stitches called *basting stitches,* in the course of the rolling the backing would slide out of place in relation to the rest of the sandwich, or get wrinkled inside the roll.

1. Press both the top and the backing, then layer and pin the sandwich.
2. Baste the sandwich in a thread whose color contrasts with that of the top so you can easily see it to pull it out later. Your basting stitches should form a 6-inch grid over the whole surface plus diagonal lines from corner to corner. Mount the basted sandwich on your frame.

3. If you're using a two-bar frame, begin quilting at the center and work your way toward the edges, rolling the quilt back and forth as needed. With a three-bar frame, begin at the bottom and work your way toward the top.

Some frames, like the one I use, have a third bar (see Chapter 1). One end of the whole sandwich is pinned to the front bar. The other end of the backing is pinned to the middle bar and the far end of the batting and top are pinned to the rear bar. In this way the backing can be stretched independently of the top, maintaining a constant tension in both. In this situation, basting is not necessary.

In the quilt I made for the demonstration, I hand quilted the squares using a pale blue thread in the "stitch-in-the-ditch" pattern on all seams to enhance the three-dimensional effect. I then quilted the border in a pattern designed to resemble a traditional style of woodwork with fluted boards and corner rosettes, using a light blue thread to emphasize the architectural detail.

Lap Quilting

This project could also be *lap-quilted,* in which the sandwich is quilted in sections. In this case a block about three squares wide and four squares long is sandwiched with batting and backing 2 inches larger on all sides. The block is pinned or basted and machine quilted or hand quilted with the "stitch-in-the ditch" pattern to within a couple of inches of the edges. Lap quilting can be done with any design that can be divided into sections of manageable size.
1. After trimming the batting to the seam line, sew the tops of the sections together.
2. Trim the backing to allow a 1/4-inch seam allowance, then smooth out the back of one section.
3. Spread over that the back of the adjacent section, turn under the seam allowance, and slipstitch the backings together.
4. Finish the quilting near the seam lines.

BINDING THE QUILT

The binding, which is red, is attached to the quilted sandwich using the method outlined for the dolls' quilts in Chapters 3 and 4. Note that the binding for this quilt is wider, a 4-inch-wide strip folded in half lengthwise, which is in proportion to its larger dimensions.

Turn to page 54 to see an entirely different use of the Attic Window pattern. In a single pane Dorothy Holden has given us a universe. I'd love to visit with Crazy Sue in the attic window.

Billy shows off the finished quilt beside his tree house.

(Right) A detail of one of the border's corners shows the quilted rosette and fluted panels that suggest woodwork.

Project: A Bargello Lap Robe

The Bargello design involves a kind of strip-quilting whose drama depends on the manipulation of values. The "secret" to making the visually complex Bargello may be revealed by looking at a short-cut method of making a checkerboard patchwork. If you piece strips of two strongly contrasting colors in alternating rows, crosscut the striped assemblage, shift alternate rows one strip, then sew those rows together—voilà! A checkerboard! By adjusting several variables—the number of fabrics, the width of the crosscuts, and the degree of shift—you end up with a Bargello design. Bargello uses as many fabrics as there are strips, makes the crosscuts of unequal width, and allows the rows to slip past each other in series.

ESTIMATING AND CUTTING THE FABRICS

For the quilt in this demonstration, I assembled an array of fabrics in a range of values, from dark purple to pale purple, then pale green to dark green, and cut a 2-inch-wide strip from each. These strips are supposed to run from selvedge to selvedge, but for many of these fabrics I didn't have full widths, so I pieced them as close to the halfway point as possible. Whether you piece an individual strip won't make a difference in a Bargello because the array has to be cut in two anyway once it's assembled.

The lab robe I made for the demonstration has a finished size of 45 by 52 inches, of which the Bargello panel occupies a space 25 by 32 inches. I used one 2-inch-wide strip, including seam allowance, of each of twenty-three fabrics. The two exceptions were the fabrics that are repeated in the triple border. I used one of these for both the backing and the binding. The inner band of the border is 1 1/2 inches wide plus seam allowance, the middle one is 3 inches wide plus seam allowance, and the outer one is 5 1/2 inches plus seam allowance. The binding has a finished width of 1/2 inch. You have learned in previous chapters how to calculate yardage for all of these, as well as the backing and batting. As for the Attic Windows bed quilt, a low-loft polyester batting is appropriate for this project.

If you want to make your quilt larger, you can either repeat some or all fabric strips, use a larger variety, or increase the width of the border. You can increase the length of the Bargello panel by adding more strips to your array. To increase its width, you are limited by the width of the yard goods, and will have to make a second array to set beside the first.

PIECING AND PRESSING

Accuracy is so critical to the effectiveness of this type of piecing that I cleaned and lubricated my sewing machine and changed the needle before starting. I also decided that I would need some kind of guide that could be attached to the needleplate so that I could make my seams as straight as possible. I searched the house for something with a sticky backing that was a little thicker than two layers of fabric, and found an adhesive-backed pad for foot calluses. I sliced it in half with the rotary cutter and stuck it to the needleplate and the base of the machine a 1/4 inch to the right of the needle. This made an 1/8-inch-high guide wall against which to align the fabric as it moves toward the needle. I have never sewn straighter seams with less effort. It was well worth the few minutes it took to set up.

1. Sew all the strips together, keeping the arrangement of values intact.

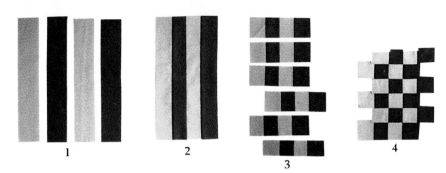

A simple and efficient way to piece a checkerboard:
1. *Alternate strips of equal length in two colors.*
2. *Sew the strips together.*
3. *Crosscut the assembled strips, then slip one row one strip in either direction.*
4. *Assemble the crosscut and shifted pieces to make a checkerboard.*

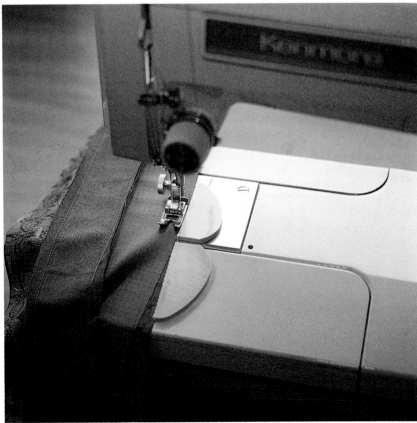

I arranged the fabrics I selected for the demonstration Bargello in a range of values, from dark purple to pale purple, from pale green to dark green.

To piece the strips of your Bargello's fabrics accurately, use two sections of foam rubber adhesive pad set 1/4 inch to the right of the needle to guide your stitches.

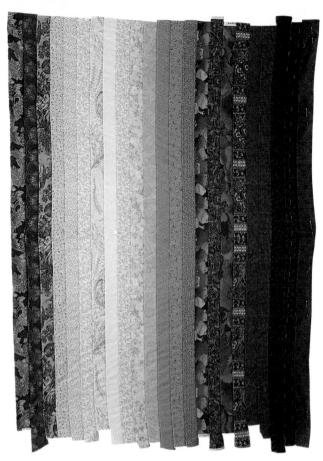

Your initial array of assembled strips won't make an impressive composition.

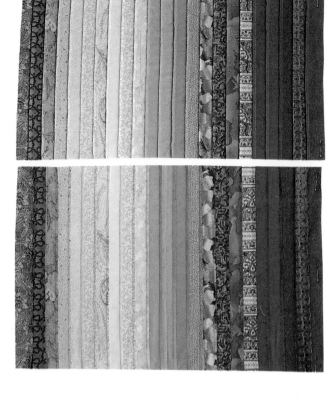

Trim the edges of the array so that they are even, then cut it approximately in half. Press the seam allowances on one section toward the right, and those on the other section toward the left.

Sew the left and right strips of each section to make tubes.

(Above) Crosscut the tubes to make loops of patches in varying widths, then open one seam in each loop to make a strip of crosscut patches.

(Right) The back of the pieced Bargello shows the alternating seam allowances.

2. Cut the assembled array roughly in half. Press the seam allowance on one half of the array up, and the seam allowance on the other down.

3. Sew the left hand stripe of each array to its right hand stripe to make tubes.

4. Crosscut the tubes to make loops of patches of varying widths. (Wide patches make shallow waves, and narrow patches make steep waves.)

5. Rip open a seam in the loop to make a strip of crosscut patches.

6. By ripping open a different seam in each loop, you shift the series of patches in whichever direction you want your Bargello design to go.

7. To avoid causing a lump of seam allowance at each intersection, assemble crosscut strips first from one tube and then from the other, pressing each seam as you go.

If you examine the photograph of the finished quilt (above), you'll see that the complexity of the design is based on variations in the width of the crosscut strips. The original fabric strips were cut 2 inches wide. They could be any width as long as they are all exactly the same. The crosscuts are the ones that should vary. Here they ranged from 1 to 2 1/2 inches in width. When the seam allowance is used up, you are left with bands ranging from a 1/2 inch to 2 inches wide.

ADDING THE BORDER AND QUILTING THE SANDWICH

Three bands compose the border here. The first, which is 1 1/2 inches wide, is the darkest purple. The second, which is 3 inches wide, is the palest purple and is quilted in roundhand script with words from Shakespeare's Sonnet 8. The text was marked on the fabric with a water-erasable blue marking pen. The third border, which is also dark, is 5 inches wide and quilted with the name of the quilt's owner, Katie, all the way around the border in gold thread. Here I used a silver pencil, which shows up clearly when marking dark colors. I machine-quilted the lines between the bands using the "stitch-in-the-ditch" pattern. I quilted the Bargello section of the top in sweeping lines crossing diagonally opposite seam intersections. These gold threads accentuate the rhythm of the Bargello.

Donna Radner's "Ocean Swirls" (see page 60) takes the Bargello design to an extreme of complexity. It's fun to study her design and try to figure out how she did it.

Project: A Medallion Shoeshine Stool

The Mariner's Compass is a popular pattern for a Medallion quilt.

The traditional Medallion quilt is one in which a complex round or oval motif is set in a background that covers most or all of the top of the bed and radiates toward its edges. Near or at those edges, a secondary pattern forms a band that falls down over the sides; this in turn is surrounded by a border. A prime example of a Medallion, and perhaps the most familiar, is the "Mariner's Compass," shown above. Except for king size, a Medallion quilt for a bed is necessarily rectangular, while one made as a pillow cover or for a wall hanging is as likely to be square.

For this demonstration, the Medallion quilt is a top for a butterprint shoeshine stool, circa 1910. The area to be covered is small—13 inches square—

so the design is simple. Every stage could be carried out full size. Even within this tiny space the same principles that are covered in the first few chapters apply.

COMPOSING THE DESIGN
This design calls for five fabrics: one dense and dark; one more open, lighter, and in a larger-scale print; one medium-dark border print; one medium-light tone-on-tone print; and one stripe in mixed tones. You can see that these basic categories leave plenty of room for choice. When you choose fabrics for your project you're sure to find some surprises that offer opportunities for changes to improve the design. Such decisions are not final until the work is

In this plan, the various values are indicated by cross-hatching and other marks.

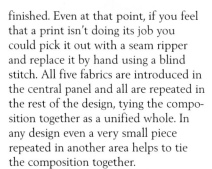

(Above) On these patterns for templates the seam allowances appear as white borders.

(Right) The fabric study of one quarter of the design is reflected in a hinged mirror.

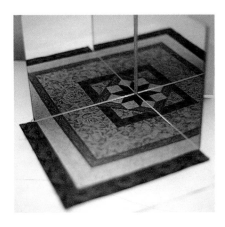

finished. Even at that point, if you feel that a print isn't doing its job you could pick it out with a seam ripper and replace it by hand using a blind stitch. All five fabrics are introduced in the central panel and all are repeated in the rest of the design, tying the composition together as a unified whole. In any design even a very small piece repeated in another area helps to tie the composition together.

1. Begin by drawing a 13-inch square. Divide it into the three classic Medallion sections: the central field, which contains the medallion; the middle band; and the border. Any traditional eight-pointed star could serve as a radiating focal motif. Since you're bound to make many changes as your design develops, make your drawing in pencil and have a good eraser handy.

2. To the heart of the star assign the densest and darkest print. This will be more dramatic statement than a pale center. I used a dark green-and-black print. Surround the central motif with the lightest light, here a pink geometric, then frame the star with a harmonizing border print in a medium value that repeats the hues of the first two fabrics.

3. Turn the pattern 45 degrees, then set it in a square parallel to the sides of the stool top. This change of direction emphasizes the radiating energy of the star. In the quilt I made for the demonstration, a deep red-and-black print marks the perimeter of the central field of the quilt. The space between the framed star and the perimeter of this section is filled with the same fabric used for the middle band.

4. The middle band uses a medium-light, single-hue, tone-on-tone fabric in a subdued print pattern, to serve as a kind of textured solid background for the central motif. I only used one fabric in this section because the work is so small. This was the only place where I could provide appreciable contrast of extent. The four large pieces, which are mitered to make this midsection, set off the tiny pieces that make up the central field and the narrow strips of the border.

5. The border consists of three bands: a

repeat of the first frame of the star, followed by a band of the pink geometric pattern, then the darkest fabric that was used for the heart of the star. The latter was also used as the cover for a welt cord, which binds the composition and stiffens the edge of the upholstery. Note that in a larger composition I would not have repeated the extreme light/dark contrast because it would detract from the central focus. Here the repetition works because the area involved is so small. Dark borders frame a composition more effectively than light ones do.

MAKING THE TEMPLATES

1. Cut apart the pieces of one quarter of your sketch, then trace each one on a sheet of paper. Draw a 1/4-inch seam allowance around each tracing. Using utility scissors, cut out these patterns and use them to make clear plastic templates. (Note that at the last minute I added 1/2 inch to the width of the outermost border to allow for contraction caused by quilting.)

2. Mark the seam allowance on the templates by sticking on 1/4-inch-wide strips of white peel-off labels. The points of the seam allowance were cut off a 1/4 inch from the tip of the seam line.

CUTTING THE FABRICS

Set the templates on the fabrics with the grain parallel to a long edge of each template. In the demonstration quilt there were two exceptions to this: the small triangles of the central field, where the short edges follow the grain; and the central diamonds, where the print of the fabric I used required that the figures all point outward, which made all the seam edges bias. If this is the case with the fabric you've chosen for your central motif, take care not to stretch the edges. Ordinarily in an eight-pointed star you would alternate straight and bias edges of the central diamonds to prevent stretching. Because the outer band of the border is directionally oriented, I cut half of each piece pointing in one direction and half pointing in the other.

MAKING A FABRIC STUDY

Because you can't tell how a fabric will work in a design until you see it in that context, you should make a fabric study. All sorts of inspirations may occur to you when you are actually handling the cloth. The study I made is the same size as the finished quilt, but I

needed to make only a quarter of the design because the effect of the whole can be seen in the hinged mirror. Remember that the pieces for a fabric study are cut without seam allowance. Cut each piece separately so that you can see the fabric through the clear plastic templates and center its print motif as needed.

Look at your fabric study with a critical eye. The contrasts of value should be well-distributed, and the place where the darkest dark meets the lightest light should occur at the center of interest. The contrast of hue, which should also be well-distributed, should be limited to a reasonable number of hues. Look for contrast of scale among the various print patterns, as well as contrast of extent between the relatively large area of the middle band and the smaller elements of the other two sections. There should be interesting variety in the directions of lines. The focal point should radiate toward the border, as it would on a traditional Medallion quilt; also, the background print should be unobtrusive, allowing the central motif to dominate the scene. This is the time to replace fabrics that do not succeed in fulfilling their objective in the design. It is the time to experiment with alternatives. You only have to pull off a swatch and glue on another.

This quilt turned out to be quite different from what I had imagined while drawing the plan, but that plan was necessary in order to determine how many fabrics and what hues, values, and general print styles would be appropriate. (With a larger Medallion you could use more background fabrics for a more elaborate effect.) Unfortunately, it was only after I had finished mounting the top that I realized I should have cut the red fabric with the scalloped leaf design pointing out rather than in. Life is not perfect.

PIECING AND PRESSING

Precision is particularly important with a geometric quilt. The photographs at right and opposite show the sequence in which the square was assembled. Remember to press each seam toward the darker fabric.

Near the end of the process, I discovered that because I had not been using the full seam allowance the top was too big. I removed the green outer border, cut the pink one to a much narrower width, then reattached the green one. This resulted in a more interesting

Assemble the center eight-pointed star by sewing pairs of patches together, then joining the pairs.

Sew square patches between points of the star.

Add a border print between the squares.

Sew triangles to the strips you have chosen for the edge of the central field. Then attach these assembled pieces to the square containing the star to make a larger square at a 45-degree angle to the smaller one.

effect because it increased the contrast of extent among the bands of the border.

When all the borders are attached, sew the mitered corners in one continuous seam using the method shown in the Attic Windows project (see pages 57–58).

ASSEMBLING AND QUILTING THE SANDWICH

For this project, I used extra-thin polyester batting and a plain muslin backing. Layer and smooth out your freshly pressed quilt top, the batting, and the backing. Pin and baste the sandwich, then lap quilt it using a straight stitch 1/8 inch inside the seam lines to delineate the three sections: the central Medallion, its surrounding band, and the border. Since the back will be inside the pillow case, it doesn't matter whether knots show. In the demonstration quilt you can easily see the outline stitching in dark green thread against the pink squares, emphasizing their position within the eight-pointed star design.

Trim the edges so that they are square, then add a wide green border. Press and trim this unit. Add narrow borders without sewing the mitered corners.

When you've finished quilting, trim the edges of the sandwich (mine was a 13 1/2-inch square). Make sure you also trim the batting to the seam line. This will reduce bulk, making it easier to add the welt cord.

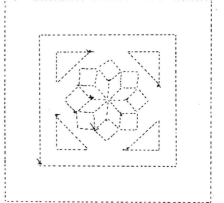

The quilting pattern shows clearly on the back.

Note in this step that the pink border has been cut to a narrower width and the mitered corners have been sewn. The welt cord is in the process of being added.

MAKING THE STOOL COVER

1. To make the welt cord for the top and bottom edges of the pad, cut about 110 inches (approximately twice the perimeter of the stool top) of 2-inch-wide bias strips of the fabric you used for the last border fabric. To make a self-covered welt cord, follow the procedure for the Pineapple Square stool cover project in Chapter 4 (see page 53).
2. Sew half of the covered cord around the seam line at the edge of the quilt

To prepare the stool top for mounting, attach strips of Velcro. Photo by Breger and Assoc., Inc.

*The finished Medallion stool.
Photo by Breger and Assoc., Inc.*

top, taking care not to stretch the cord too tightly at the corners. Trim the seam allowance to 1/4 inch, then add the sides.

3. To make the sides of the padded top of the stool, use a 1-inch-wide strip of the same fabric as the welt cord. This is also sewn onto the seam line at the edge of the quilt top right over the welt cord, forming a right angle to the top.

4. Attach the rest of the welt cord to the lower edge of the sides.

ASSEMBLING THE PAD

1. Cut two pieces of dark fabric 13 1/2 by 8 inches to serve as a bottom for the pad cover.

2. Hem one long edge of each piece, then sew the fuzzy side of a piece of Velcro tape to the right side just inside the unhemmed seam lines. (If you won't be mounting your pillow on a stool, skip this step.)

3. Using the zipper foot attachment to accommodate the welt cord, sew the pad backing and corded sides right sides together, leaving the hemmed edges of the backing as an open slit down the middle to receive the pillow.

4. Turn the case right side out, exposing the fuzzy Velcro. Cover a 1 by 13 by 13 inch polyfoam pad with unbleached muslin, then stuff it into the quilted case.

MOUNTING THE FINISHED STOOL COVER

Glue and staple the hook side of the Velcro to the edges of the stool top and attach the pad to the stool by aligning the Velcro strips.

If you would rather make a pillow with your quilted Medallion top, simply omit the sides and second cord and close the slit in the back with Velcro or a zipper.

To make a wall hanging, omit the sides and second cord and use a single piece for the back. Sew Velcro along the top edge, then glue and staple the hook side to a strip of wooden lattice. A pair of screw eyes attached to the lattice could serve as hangers.

In "Found: Directions," Michelle Vernon has created a modern Medallion using cottons, silk organza, metallic thread, acrylic paint, and laser printing. She says that she designed this quilt as the companion to her "Lost" quilt: "Both pieces explore the problem of depression and its treatment. In 'Lost' the compass is broken; in 'Found,' it has been reassembled, and the background is organized more coherently."

FOUND DIRECTIONS
by Michelle Vernon. 55 × 55 inches.
*This quilt, which is one of a series, is a contemporary Medallion design that expresses the resolution of a personal dilemma.
Photo by Breger and Assoc., Inc.*

A HAPPY THOUGHT

Once upon a time there was
a man who lied.

So his most prized possession
turned black and fell off.

Then he died.

And his wife lived happily
ever after.

is
He a Snake in
the grass

My FATHER says that
getting a DIVORCE is the
most incredibly SELFISH thing
I have ever done in my life
and my CHILDREN will grow up
to HATE me for it.

CHAPTER 6

APPLIQUÉ

ppliqué is defined as the process of applying fabric cutouts to a piece of cloth that serves as a background. In this chapter, the first project, an angel on a pillow, is a sampler of appliqué techniques: paper basting for the head, needle turn followed by satin stitch for the halo, fusible webbing and machine appliqué for the dress, buttonhole stitch for the lace hem, and hidden appliqué for the hands and arms. The African print banner is reversible, with text on both sides appliquéd by machine. The Indonesian footstool has a stuffed motif appliquéd by hand.

(Opposite) THE DIVORCE QUILT by Katharine Brainard.
This work expresses strong feelings in a humorous way.
(Above) The staff of Beacon House with one of the children they are helping to raise.

Appliqué Techniques

The most common methods for appliqué are outlined below and illustrated in the "Angelface" pillow cover on the opposite page. Reverse appliqué can be seen in the detail of the iris on the antique quilt below, right.

One problem that tends to arise with any appliqué technique is the undesired thickness that is a result of a buildup of layers of fabric. To reduce this, you could use an 1/8-inch seam allowance and trim away underlying layers where pieces overlap.

BASIC PROCEDURE

1. On a sheet of tracing paper, trace either a found or an original image.
2. Transfer the image to sketching paper. Mark each segment of the image with a line parallel to the edge of the composition. This will be the grain line of the cut fabric, which should be aligned with the grain of the background fabric.
3. Cut out each segment of the paper image separately. Mark the right side of segments that are asymmetrical.
4. Cut the background fabric, allowing for reduction caused by quilting. If you're using a light-colored fabric, spread it right side up over the traced design. Using a pencil, trace 1/16 inch within each shape. If you can't see the pattern through the fabric, tape both the tracing paper (first) and the fabric to a window. The daylight will illuminate the tracing from behind, making it easier to see through the cloth. You could also use a lightbox.
5. Cut out all segments of the image, adding 1/4-inch seam allowance. For narrow linear pieces such as flower stems, a special tool called a Fasturn, available in most quilting stores, makes bias tubes from strips of bias fabric.

At this point in the process, you could use any of the appliqué procedures described below.

Paper Basting

1. Spread the paper pattern on the wrong side of the fabric shape. Fold the seam allowance over the paper pattern and baste. Press the wrong side, then the right side. (Refer to step 1 of the sampler.)
2. Set the pressed piece with its paper lining in the proper place on the background fabric with the straight grain matched. Pieces that will be overlapped by others go on first, followed by the foreground pieces. Pin and then baste these 1/4 inch from the edges.
3. Using a slipstitch or whipstitch, sew each piece to the background fabric, taking care not to catch the paper lining with your needle. Leave a 1/2 inch open. Remove the basting threads, pull out the paper pattern with tweezers, and sew up the remaining 1/2 inch. (Refer to step 3 of the sampler.)

Fusible Webbing

A second method is to use fusible webbing in place of the paper. This product is available in fabric stores and comes with instructions for bonding to the cutout and then to the background fabric. (See steps 1 and 3 of the sampler.)

Hidden Appliqué

This approach involves sewing by hand or machine a lining of lightweight fabric to each cutout piece right sides together along seam lines. Clip the curves and Vs, cut a slit in the lining, and pull the piece right side out through the slit. The resulting lined piece is then pressed so that the seam is aligned precisely at the edges. This hides the seam allowance inside. The piece is then applied to the background. (See steps 1 and 4 of the sampler.)

Needle Turn Appliqué

Clip curves to 1/16 inch from the seam line. Use a single strand of thread and hide the knot inside the seam allowance. Turn the seam allowance under with your needle and hold it in place with the thumb of your other hand while sewing the piece on with a blindstitch or a whipstitch. (See step 2 of the sampler.)

Embroidery Appliqué

In addition to the blindstitch and the whipstitch, cutouts can be appliquéd by hand or embellished afterward using various embroidery stitches, such as blanket stitch, herringbone, and lazy daisy. For a chart of embroidery stitches, refer to pages 88–89. (See step 4 of the sampler.)

Machine Topstitching

The sturdiest appliqué is done by machine using a medium-width zigzag stitch set on the shortest stitch length. (See steps 3 and 4 of the sampler.)

Reverse Appliqué

In this method, the design is cut into the background fabric and contrasting smaller pieces are set behind the holes and blindstitched in place. Variations of reverse appliqué have been used all over the world. The *molas* that are made by the Indians of the San Blas Islands and the images by the Hmong people of Laos, many of whom are now working among the Amish quilters of Pennsylvania, are but two examples. (See the details of the antique quilt, below.)

(Top) In this detail of a quilt by Martha Jane Neal Craven, circa 1920, you can see how the reverse appliqué was constructed. The shapes are cut in the background fabric, seam allowances tucked under, and the colored fabric set behind the hole. (Above) An unfinished part of the same quilt top, as seen from the back.

"ANGELFACE" PILLOW COVER APPLIQUÉ SAMPLER

Step 1. (Upper left) The halo has been notched all around the curve and the paper pattern placed over the wrong side. I used a double layer of yellow fabric so that the dark background would not show through. (Upper right) The seam allowance of the face cut-out has been pressed over the paper and basted. (Lower left) A lining has been sewn to the hands and arms along the seam lines. (Lower right) A fusible webbing has been pressed onto the dress, the paper layer partly peeled away, and part of the seam allowance fused to the webbing.

Step 2. Part of the seam allowance is turned under and held in place with a thumb while slipstitching the edge in place.

Step 3. At this stage, the wings have been basted and straight machine-stitched in place. The face has been slipstitched over the halo, the basting threads removed, and the tweezers are pulling the paper lining out. The body has been fused in place over wings and a lace hem, then straight machine-stitched 1/8 inch inside the edge.

Step 4. The completed pillow cover. The halo was satin-stitched in gold thread by machine. The hands were slipstitched in place and the hem was blanket-stitched by hand in gold. The lace motif was embroidered in gold with a lazy daisy stitch, the eyes and mouth embroidered, and the hair sewn on with beads in the braids. The braids are made of three strands of yarn, and the beads, which were added after braiding, were sewn on with black thread. The pleats in the wings were secured with blanket stitching in white thread.

The "Angelface" pillow. The background fabric, from Dakar, Senegal, West Africa, has a triadic color scheme of red-violet, green, and yellow. The first two colors are repeated in the hair beads, and the third in the halo.

1

2

3

4

Project: A Reversible Appliquéd Banner

The proverb that inspired this design expresses a truth of which we all need to be reminded. It is acted upon every day at Beacon House, a Unitarian community ministry in northeast Washington, D.C. Refer to page 71 to see the banner displayed by the staff of Beacon House with one of the many children they are helping to raise. The man in the clerical collar is the Reverend Mr. Don Robinson, founder of Beacon House and one of my personal heroes.

CHOOSING THE FABRICS

The proverb appliquéd to this banner, which measures 26 by 38 inches, is African in origin, so I selected a traditional African print made in the Ivory Coast. It has a strong design and a vivid combination of hues, so the lettering fabric had to be fairly plain, in this case yellow with orange rectangles, echoing two of the colors in the print. The cloth I chose for the reverse side of the banner is a solid blue that matches the blue of the print.

The sentiments in your banner can be expressed with text, by an image, or with a combination of both. One of the advantages of making a banner or a wall hanging is that you're not confined to a certain size or shape. (A banner has to be reversible; a wall hanging does not.)

CUTTING THE FABRICS

The layout of the banner that I made for the demonstration takes advantage of the design of the background fabric. The stepped edge along the bottom follows the outlines of the print, and I used letters the same height as its squares. I cut a second panel exactly the same shape as the first from the solid blue fabric for the reverse side. To make templates for the letters, I traced 3-inch-high commercial peel-off letters on old manila file folders, then cut the fabrics 1/8 inch outside the traced edge.

MACHINE APPLIQUÉ

1. For the print side of the banner, I cut two sets of yellow letters and sewed them on double thickness so that they would hide the vivid colors underneath. If your fabric ravels easily, use Fray Check to keep the cut edges intact.
2. I used a straight machine stitch around the edges of the letters, then separated them visually from the background by covering the edges of each one with a heavy black line of satin stitch. This line sharpens their character, giving them the strength to hold their place in the design. Regardless of its message or content, in a banner you need to define edges clearly so that your statement will be evident even from a distance.
3. The solid blue on the reverse side carries the same words, which I cut from the African print fabric. I marked the location of the base lines of the letters in white chalk by spreading the blue fabric over the print and feeling the lumps made by the letters on the reverse. I deliberately included in one of the "I"s the fabric's country of origin, *Côte d'Ivoire* (Ivory Coast). I then outlined these letters in white satin stitch to strengthen their contrast with the dark background.

ASSEMBLING AND QUILTING THE SANDWICH

1. After I had finished the lettering, I made the sandwich in an unorthodox way because the banner is reversible. I spread one side face up on the table, the other side over it face down, and on top of these, the batting. (The batting I used is an ultrathin, nonbearding polyester product called Thermore, made by Hobbs Bonded Fibers. It's very easy to handle, with just the right bulk for this project.)
2. Once I had aligned and pinned the layers, I machine stitched along the seam lines of the bottom and the sides, leaving the top 3 inches or so of the sides open.
3. I turned the sandwich right side out and pressed the edges. I then turned under the seam allowances of the side openings and top stitched them 1/8 inch from the edge. I sewed the seam across the top of the banner as well as the rest of the side seams and the bottom with a top stitch.
4. I pinned the sandwich every 6 inches. Since the same letters did not align back to back, I quilted around them following the white lines on the printed design. I used yellow thread in the bobbin and white thread on top so that the yellow thread shows up well against the dark blue, echoing the line design of the patterned fabric, but the white thread disappears against the white lines of the African print. In designing your quilting pattern, take into consideration how it will look on both sides.

FINISHING THE BANNER

No binding was necessary because the edges are enclosed in seams. The 3-inch openings that I left at the top of each side seam (see step 2, above) allow a dowel to be slipped through for hanging. A gold thread tied to both ends of the dowel completes the work. If you're making a wall hanging instead of a banner, refer to the Memorial Quilt Triptych project, page 127, for recommendations on hanging.

Making this banner was a way for me to express an idea about which I feel strongly. Katharine Brainard used quilting as a means for releasing quite different feelings with humor. "The Divorce Quilt" (see page 70) has become famous from coast to coast. Ms. Brainard says, "It was cathartic; a healing quilt," and "The wonderful thing is I don't feel this way anymore."

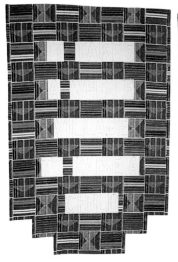

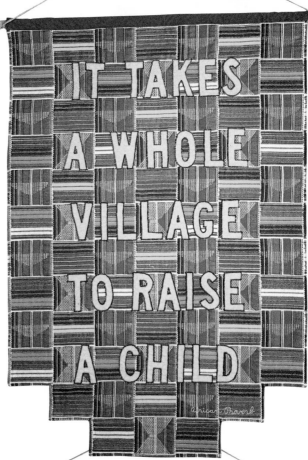

I blocked out the spacing of the words.

I mounted the yellow lettering on the African print fabric.

The yellow letters are set off clearly by the black stitching around their edges.

I then blocked out areas for lettering on the blue fabric for the reverse of the banner.

The lettering also shows up well on the back of the banner.

Yellow quilting lines on the blue side of the banner echo the print pattern of the African fabric. The rod is a standard 1/2-inch dowel with grooves cut around each end to keep the gold cord from slipping off.

Project: A Hand Appliquéd Footstool

I upholstered the Indonesian footstool shown at right as a graduation present for my nephew, Edward Crooke, who was about to furnish his own apartment. Its appliquéd design was sewn by hand. In contrast to the machine appliqué illustrated in the African print banner, where the stitching is part of the design, in this technique the stitching is carefully hidden. For your stool you could use any of the hand appliqué methods described earlier in this chapter (see pages 72–73).

The dimension of the footstool is 8 inches high, 9 inches wide, and 12 inches long. The top is a high-crowned oval cushion that was originally upholstered in white damask. When estimating fabric for your footstool, use a tape measure to get the longest length and widest width, including the depth of the top. For such a small project you can estimate your yardage very generously. For different-shaped stool tops, refer to the Pineapple Square stool cover project in Chapter 4 and the Medallion shoeshine stool project in Chapter 5.

CREATING, CUTTING, AND HANDSTITCHING THE APPLIQUÉ

1. For this demonstration I began by making a pencil rubbing of the hand-carved frame and legs of the stool. I adapted some of the carved shapes to

This footstool with handcarved frame and legs was upholstered in an impractical white damask.

I made a pencil rubbing of the wood carving and adapted it as a pattern for the appliqué design.

I basted the oval piece from which the border and initials were to be cut to the background fabric.

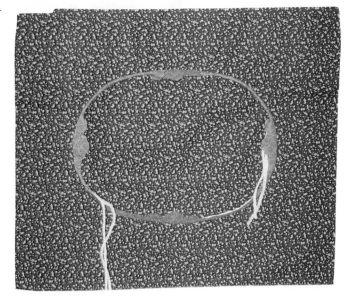

I stuffed the border with strands of yarn.

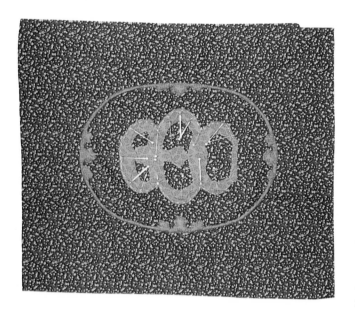

I used yarn and bits of polyfil as stuffing for the initials.

I quilted the top on a diagonal grid between the initials and the border.

use as the basis of an oval arrangement of Eddy's initials, then added a border that echoed both the oval and the carving. The repetition of design elements unifies the frame and the top of the footstool.

2. I marked a 1/4-inch seam allowance around the outside of the border and used this drawing as a pattern for cutting an oval of tone-on-tone rust-colored fabric. I turned under the seam allowance around the perimeter, basted it with white thread, and pressed it. Then I centered this on a 12 by 18 inch piece of green-and-brown printed fabric and slipstitched using the tiniest possible stitches in matching thread.

3. I marked the inside edge of the border design on the appliquéd oval, marked the seam allowance, then cut away the center of the oval so I could use it later for the initials. I clipped all the inner curves of the border, turned them under, and basted the seam allowance.

STUFFING THE APPLIQUÉ

To emphasize the contrast between the appliqué and the background, I decided to stuff the cutout with yarn.

1. After spreading several lengths of yarn between the appliqué and the background fabric, I began to sew the inside edge to the background with more tiny stitches. I sewed a short distance, stuffed a little more of the appliqué, then sewed some more, until the whole border was stuffed and sewn onto the background fabric.

2. I cut out the initials and sewed them onto the green fabric in much the same manner, stuffing as I went. Where the initials overlapped, I indented the line with minute stitches. Unfortunately, as I stitched I absentmindedly boxed myself into a position where it was impossible to continue to push the stuffing in. It wasn't easy to rip out all those minute stitches but it had to be done.

ASSEMBLING AND QUILTING THE SANDWICH

The sandwich was composed of the top with its stuffed appliqué, extra-thin polyester batting, and unbleached muslin. I lap-quilted the background fabric on a diagonal grid marked with white chalk, leaving the thread ends dangling on the right side. The thread matches the dark green because the print is so busy that contrasting thread would have been too distracting.

MOUNTING THE QUILT TOP

Using a staple gun with small staples, I fastened the quilt to the frame of the stool once at each end and midway on each side. Then I pulled the loose ends of the quilting threads to gather the top evenly down over the sides of the padded part of the stool. I finished stapling all around and trimmed the edges of the quilt close to the edge of the carving. Using a low-temperature glue gun (available in craft stores), I glued on braided trim to match the golden brown print on the green fabric.

"Pinnately and Bi-Pinnately" by Jeanne Benson is a masterful specimen of hand appliqué worthy of careful study.

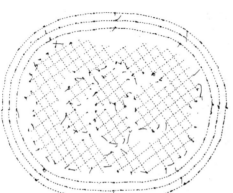

On the back of the quilt top, the thread lengths on the three lines around the border are quite short. Their ends hang loose on the other side so that when the quilt is positioned on top of the stool the outer edges can be gathered evenly down over the convex surface.

One quarter of the top has been gathered, stapled, and trimmed.

The quilt was gathered snugly and stapled on all sides, then the braid was glued around the raw edges. Photo by Breger and Assoc., Inc.

PINNATELY AND BI-PINNATELY (DETAIL) by Jeanne Benson. 1993. 23 × 37 inches.
*This quilt, which expresses the artist's interest in delicate botanical forms, is an
exquisite example of hand appliqué. Photo by Breger and Assoc., Inc.*

Pieced in 1910 by
Martha Jane Neal Craven,
Great, great grandmother of Wendy Grubbs.
Embroidered in 1994 especially for Wendy
by his granny, Daisy Grubbs.

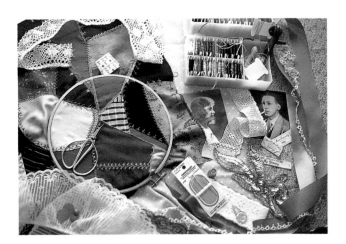

CHAPTER 7

EMBROIDERED CRAZY QUILTS

razy quilts are not meant to be made in a hurry, like a "quilt-in-a-day." The process is more like doodling with needle and thread, pure fun. The design of these quilts reflects the era in which they were first made, as Victorian society was one in which women had the leisure to embellish and the means to collect fancy fabrics, trim, and mementos of historical and personal events. Elaborate design characterized every aspect of the lives of those who had time to spare. These quilts were for display rather than utility, which is why they don't require batting. 🐦 Today few of us have much leisure but small crazy quilts require less of that. This chapter offers several examples that demonstrate the process without requiring a great investment of time. Bear in mind that just as the cigarette silks, cigar bands, souvenir ribbons, embroidered initials, handkerchiefs, and handmade laces of Victorian crazy quilts are historical artifacts, so your crazy quilts can preserve something of your own period.

(Opposite) A crazy quilt square pillow cover featuring appliquéd and embroidered butterflies.
(Above) The tools and ingredients for a crazy quilt.

Project: A Modern Crazy Quilt Pillow

A crazy quilt square pillow cover embroidered with proverbs.

The first of these small quilts is a cover for a 16-inch square pillow. The method involves sewing scraps to a foundation, in this case an 18-inch square of muslin. The extra 2 inches is for the seam allowance and the possible decrease in size caused by the needlework. Unlike appliqué, it doesn't matter whether the scraps are bias; the muslin will stabilize them. Among my collection of five-cent patches was a parrot that I used as the dominant feature of the square I made for the demonstration.

PIECING ON A FOUNDATION
1. On a sheet of paper, cut a five-sided window a little larger than your central motif. If you were to begin with a rectangle you would end up with another Log Cabin design. Five sides offer starting lines for strips of fabric going off in odd directions. In the project I made

for the demonstration I placed the parrot above and to the right of the center right side up and used a dark patch of green in the middle to give weight to the design. I placed the green right side down over the parrot with one edge of each aligned.
2. To add each patch, sew along the aligned seam, fold the added piece out to expose the right side, and press. When I added the sixth piece, a bright blue solid, which was the start of the second band of patches around the parrot, I was stuck with a V-shaped angle to fill. I solved that problem by adding a series of triangles called a *fan* to fill the angle. I sewed two scraps together rather than attach just one long strip to the straight line formed by the first row of patches beneath the parrot.
When your muslin base is covered, check to see that the prominent print

patterns are distributed fairly evenly over the square, the solid colors are well scattered, and the light and dark values are pretty well balanced. Take into account the distribution of each color, so that all the pinks are not on one side and all the greens on another.

EMBELLISHMENT
The embroidery is designed to help balance the distribution of lights and darks and the various hues. Note that all the seam lines on the demonstration square are straight. I cut the patches that way to simplify the process. If you use curved edges, you have to turn them under, press, baste, and hand appliqué (see page 72). I introduced some strong curves in the embroidery; for example, the pale green vine with button flowers on the lower right and the spider web, a popular Victorian motif, on the left. I

made the spider's little fat body out of a knot of black yarn. I chain-stitched the legs with a single strand of embroidery floss, and made the eyes from clear glass beads. Her name, of course, is Charlotte. For the web I used a metallic thread in the same value of green as the two adjacent fabrics.

If you were to make a bed quilt, lap robe, or wall hanging, you would add a backing but possibly not batting since the top is already two layers thick and heavily embellished. It could be tied or quilted, whichever seems appropriate.

COMPLETING THE PILLOW

1. I framed the square with a German cotton velvet that I washed and pressed beforehand. Its rich black nap sets off the colored patches like jewels on a black velvet tray.

2. I made the back of the pillow cover from two lengths of pink-and-black fabric, and for the closure I used a strip of Velcro. I spread the assembled back over the crazy quilt, right sides together, then joined the two layers around the outer seam line of the velvet frame. I opened the Velcro, turned the case right side out, and pressed the edges. I machine stitched in the ditch where the crazy quilt square meets the velvet border, making a flat frame around the plump pillow.

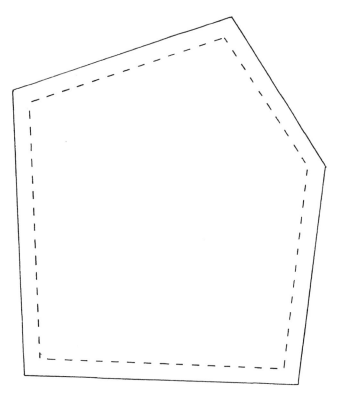

On this template for the first patch of the crazy quilt, the dotted line is the seam line, the solid line is the cutting line, and the space between the two lines is the seam allowance.

Baste your first patch onto a muslin backing 2 inches larger in length and width than the intended final dimensions. In my square the parrot dominates the design and sets the color scheme.

Set your second patch on top of the first, right sides together, with the edges to be stitched aligned.

After stitching the first seam, press it open.

Add a third patch in the same way you added the second.

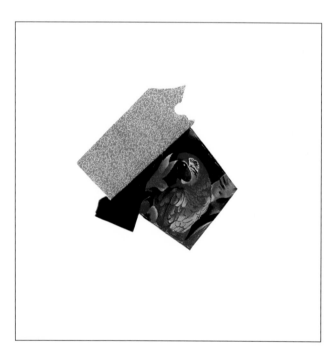 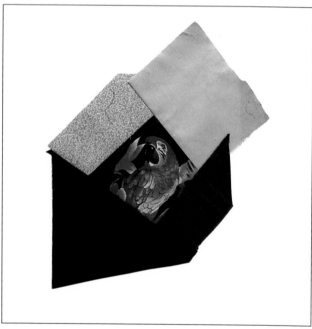

Press open the third patch after stitching.

Continue adding patches clockwise around the first.

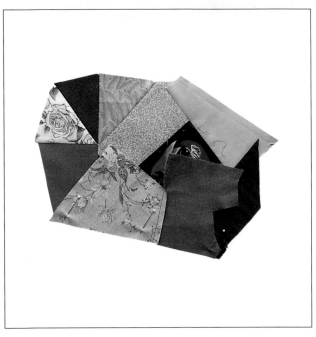

*If you create a **V**-shaped space, you can fill it with a fan of triangles. Turn and pin under the second side of the last one, and appliqué by hand.*

If you run across a long, straight edge, sew together a strip of pieces and add them as one.

Cover the entire square with scraps in a spiral pattern. Be careful to distribute values, hues, prints, and solids fairly evenly.

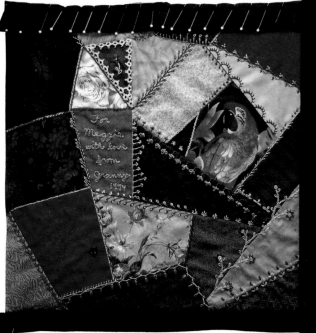

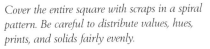

You can use embroidery to improve the balance of values and hues. Here two of the black velvet bands for a border have been stitched in place and a third pinned. Note how the print design in the upper left corner of this example echoes the feeling of the spider web.

If you're adding a border, trim the top, add 1¹/₂-inch framing strips, and fold the square in preparation for stitching the mitered corners. Here you can see that the line of basting is out of the way of the stitching line, which is an extension of the fold line.

Here the frame is finished, the backing added, and the pillow case turned right side out and pressed.

The back of the finished pillow shows the line of the Velcro closing.

A line of stitching where the velvet meets the patchwork creates a flat frame that stands out around the bulging pillow. Photo by Breger and Assoc., Inc.

GLOSSARY OF EMBROIDERY STITCHES

1. Back Stitch. Start at the right, pulling the thread through from the back. Take a running stitch and come up one stitch length from the first stitch. Put the needle back through the end of the first stitch and come up a stitch length beyond the end of the second, back through the end of the second. Repeat.

2. Buttonhole or Blanket Stitch. Start at the left, pulling up from the back on the line. Take a vertical stitch down from above the line, coming out on the line and inside the loop that is formed. When this is repeated with very close stitches it is called a *button-hole stitch*. When there is more space between the loops it is called a *blanket stitch*. Both the height and the slant of the stitches can be varied, and the base line can be curved or scalloped. The vertical stitches can alternate above and below the line, either singly or in groups.

3. Bullion Knot. This is harder to describe than to do. Pull the thread through from the back. Coming back up the first hole but without pulling the thread through, take a fairly long stitch. Wrap the thread around the point of the needle six or eight times. Holding the twists in place, pull the needle and thread through them. Push the needle and thread back through the fabric at the second hole and pull it snug.

4. Chain Stitch. Start at the right. Come up and back down through the same hole in the fabric, leaving a loose loop on top. Come up through the loop one stitch length along the line. Pull the thread snug. Go back down through the hole inside the loop, leaving a second loose loop on top. Repeat.

5. Chevron Stitch. Start at the left above the line. Take a stitch to the right, but come back up to the left under the middle of the first stitch. Take a long diagonal stitch down and to the right. Go through the fabric below the line and come up a half stitch length to the left. Take a full stitch right over this half stitch. Go down through the fabric and come up again a half stitch to the left. Take a long diagonal stitch up above the line to the right. Repeat.

6. Couching. Place one long thread or bundle of threads along a line. Attach it to the fabric with another matching or contrasting thread by taking very small stitches over the straight thread at equal intervals along the line.

7. Cretan Stitch. Start at the left. Come up from the back and move diagonally up toward the right. Take a small vertical stitch down, coming out still above the line and inside the loop of thread. Pull it snug. Turn the needle to take a vertical stitch upward from below the line and come out still below the line, to the right, and inside the second loop. Pull the thread snug and repeat.

8. Cross Stitch. These stitches usually occur in groups. Start at the right and make parallel diagonal stitches for the number of crosses required. Then go back the other way crossing each half stitch and using the same holes.

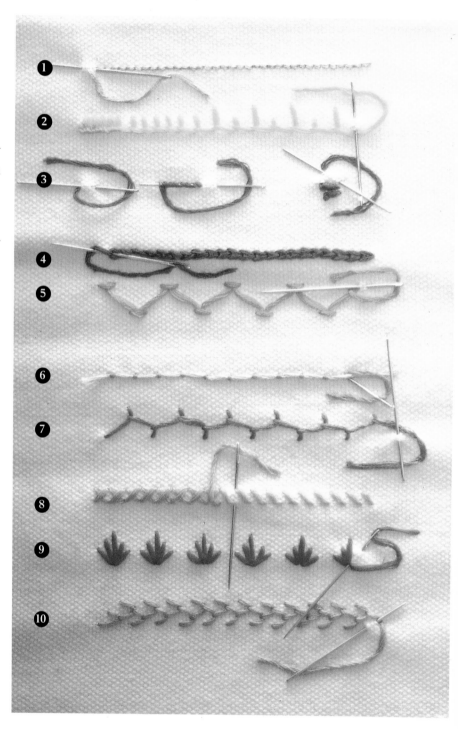

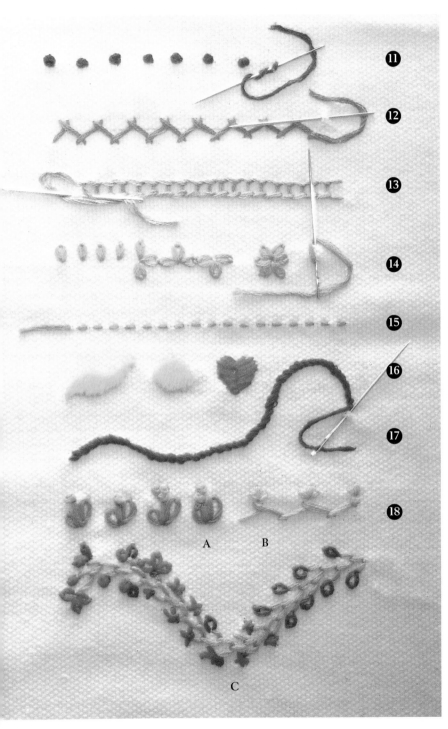

9. Fans. Pull the needle through from the back of the fabric at the base of the fan. Take a long diagonal stitch toward the left, then follow it with four more stitches that all share the same bottom hole and fan out to the right. The middle stitch should be the longest. Fans can also be made of lazy daisy stitches, and turned in any direction.

10. Feather Stitch. Start at the top. Pull the needle through from the back and return a stitch length to the right, leaving a loose loop. Pull the needle through again from the back through the bottom of the loop, forming a **V**. Push the needle through to the back a stitch length to the right and level with the base of the **V**, leaving a loose loop. Repeat to the left under the first **V**, then again to the right under the second **V**, and so on.

11. French Knot. Pull the needle through from the back. Wrap the thread around the needle twice and, holding the floss snug, slip the point of the needle back close to the same hole. Hold the knot while pulling the thread through to the back.

12. Herringbone Stitch. Start at the left above the line with a small horizontal back stitch. Move to the right and take another small horizontal back stitch below the line. Move above the line again and to the right. Repeat.

13. Ladder Stitch. Starting at the right, pull the needle through from the back. Push the needle again to the back above the point where you brought the needle up, leaving a loose loop to the left. Come back up through the loop a stitch length to the left of the first hole. Leave the first loop loose enough to push the needle back through it a stitch length to the left of the upper hole, leaving a second loop. Repeat.

14. Lazy Daisy. Bring the needle up from the back and return it through the same hole, leaving a loop. Bring the needle back up through the loop a stitch away. Pull the loop snug, cross over it, and return to the back with a tiny stitch to hold the loop in place.

15. Running Stitch. Make small even stitches with spaces between them equal to their length.

16. Satin Stitch. This is a series of parallel stitches close together to fill an outlined area. The stitches can be horizontal, vertical, or diagonal.

17. Stem Stitch. Start at the left (if you are right-handed) and take small slightly overlapping stitches, keeping the thread to the left of the needle. The effect will be like rope.

18. Combinations. You can combine embroidery stitches for greater variety. The examples shown are:

A. Unequal lazy daisies with a straight stitch between them and French knots.

B. Herringbone stitches with abbreviated fans.

C. Feather stitches with lazy daisies, French knots, small single stitches, and abbreviated fans.

(Above) The backs of five of the old squares, two different blue checks, one blue plaid, one solid blue, and a piece of an Anderson Feed sack reveal as much about their time in history as do their pieced tops.

(Left) On this basted square by Martha Craven, note the odd shapes and angles, the balance of lights and darks and patterns and solids, and the somberness of the colors.

Around 1910, my husband's grandmother, Martha Jane Neal Craven, made a collection of crazy quilt squares roughly 18 inches on a side. She embroidered only a few of them. In the early 1970s my mother-in-law, Fay Craven Grubbs, passed these squares on to me. I added to the embroidery at that time but never assembled them into the bed quilt for which they may have been intended. Instead, I decided to divide them among Martha Craven's descendants and make several small keepsakes.

Martha had pieced these antique squares by hand, appliquéing each scrap onto the backing fabric with tiny stitches, resulting in great variety of line and form. The tops are composed of velvet, velveteen, satin, taffeta, and a number of ribbons. The fabrics she used as backing are just as interesting. The most commonly available fabrics seem to have been old worn house dresses and feed sacks.

If you have or can find some pieces of old crazy quilt, you might want to incorporate them into a table runner, a piano throw, or a panel of a jacket, dress, or evening bag.

C O L O R   N O T E

ORCHESTRATING COMBINATIONS OF FABRIC AND FINDINGS

Most of the colors of these antique squares are subdued and pleasantly mellow. I used a neutral tone of brown for the family tree wall hanging so that it would not compete with the old fabrics and to let the bright embroidery floss attract attention to the names.

For the lap quilt/wall hanging, the black velvet is the densest dark value possible in fabric. It presents a stunning contrast with the embroidered squares as well as with the jewel-like Thai silk border and backing.

The feline-theme pillow benefits from contrast with black velvet-covered welt cord. As with all crazy quilting, each floss, bead, and button is carefully chosen to create contrast in some way with the fabric behind it.

A FAMILY TREE WALL HANGING

I made the first of these keepsakes for Martha's great-great-granddaughter, Rachel, who lives in Switzerland and seldom sees the American side of her family. For that reason I chose to design a family tree to appliqué onto one of the squares. I intended that the finished piece would be framed and hung on a wall.

Realizing an Idea

I sketched a tree with thick branches to accommodate the names of Rachel's ancestors. I arranged Martha's side of the family dating back to her generation on the left side of the tree and the Swiss family to the same generation on the right. Rather than middle names I included maiden names to clarify the relationships. Since I am a stepmother and not in the bloodline, I appear as a flower at the base of the tree.

Correcting the Inevitable Problems

1. At first I embroidered the family names all in green, assigning the strongest shade to Rachel's name and making each preceding generation progressively paler. As you can see in the photograph at the top of page 92, this was a mistake—the names were barely legible. Moreover, the names of the quilt's makers—mine and Martha's—were much too prominent. Every single one had to be done over again. This was a case of "haste makes waste," but it was a valuable lesson. On the finished piece each generation is stitched in a different hue and the names of the quilters are suitably subdued.

2. The square that I used for this project had a piece missing along the bottom edge. I covered the area with part of a strip of eyelet—modern, machine-made, stark white. The extreme contrast with the dense black piece immediately to the right called attention to that spot, which was of no compositional interest. On impulse I scribbled on the eyelet with a blue felt-tip pen whose ink proved to be nonpermanent. I dabbed it with a damp paper towel and made a mess. Frantic blotting removed most of the blue and luckily didn't stain any of the other pieces or the backing. The white had become less bright, but there was still too much contrast, so I covered the area with a mediating border of purple blanket stitch. The final effect is interesting without being too obtrusive.

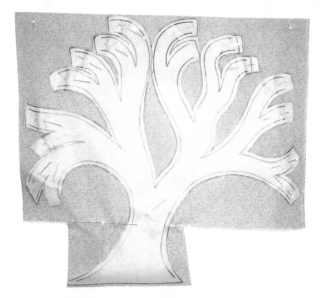

I cut the pattern for a family tree from tracing paper and spread it on a light tone-on-tone print.

I pinned the tree with embroidered names to the square, seam allowance turned under.

I hand-appliquéd the tree to the square.

91

Final Embellishments

1. I added a variety of beads, buttons, and embroidery.
2. I filled the space between the two main branches with a snapshot of Rachel printed on fabric. I took the photograph and a small piece of plain white fabric to a local photocopying shop. They made a color photocopy of the picture from which they made a color print on the white cloth. Another easy process for reproducing a photo is called *sunprinting*. An undyed cotton fabric is painted with a chemical solution, dried in a dark room, pressed, and sandwiched with a contact negative between cardboard and glass. The package is then exposed to the sun until a blue print emerges. Modifying the chemical solution produces different hues. Shown on the opposite page is a sunprint quilt by Susan Johnson. (Refer to the Sources on page 142 for a supplier of chemicals and related materials.) You can also copy images onto fabric with transfer medium, available in most fabric stores.
3. I cropped the fabric around the photographic image, slipped the edges under some seams in the crazy quilt square, and embroidered around it. I hand-appliquéd an iridescent ribbon border approximately the color of the tree around the hanging after the quilt was trimmed square.

(Above) Here the embroidery is finished and the ribbon binding sewn halfway around the square. The names on the tree are too pale and the quilters' names too bright. The emphasis should be reversed.

A snapshot of Rachel commands the center of the finished piece. I re-embroidered all the names so that the ones on the tree dominate the composition and the quilters' names are subordinate.

Sunprinting can be done with silhouettes as in this quilt by Susan Johnson.

A LAP QUILT/WALL HANGING

My second collaboration with Martha Craven was for another of her great-great-granddaughters, Eowyn. I chose three of the antique squares and with some trepidation cut each into four smaller squares to make a set of twelve. My hesitation to cut was overcome by the thought that if I did nothing with them they might never be seen and enjoyed by others. By adding sashes and borders, I could expand twelve small squares into a larger and better proportioned shape than I could create with three large ones.

Cutting and Organizing the Squares

1. When I first received the squares I embroidered Martha Craven's name and mine in the center of the upper half of one of the larger ones. As a result, I had to cut it so that the names would be centered on a smaller square, and then join the sections that I had trimmed from each side to form another. After cutting and repiecing the squares, I embroidered any seams that I had not covered earlier.

2. I pinned the twelve squares onto the felt wall in my studio, rearranging them several times to distribute the darks and striking colors evenly over the whole area of the top. I placed the signature square on the lower right.

Adding the Sashes and Borders

1. I had a little over a yard of 60-inch-wide velvet for the sashes and borders. In order to make them as wide as possible and to be sure that the nap would all run in the same direction, I made a scale layout on paper before cutting the velvet, and found that 3 1/2-inch-wide sashes and 4-inch-wide borders would be the maximum sizes obtainable.

2. I don't usually baste, but with velvet it is essential. The nap creeps relentlessly unless it is tightly basted. When I had sewn all the vertical sashes to the squares, I added the longer horizontal ones, then the borders around the outside of the assembled pieces.

Finishing the Quilt

1. So that they would stand out brilliantly against the enveloping black, I added a line of chain stitching around the perimeter of every square, using a different color for each one.

2. For the backing I used a medium-weight silk from Thailand. It has a slightly rough texture and is iridescent, black warp crossed by peacock blue woof. I smoothed the top over the silk backing and tied the two layers together at each corner of every square using six-strand black floss that vanishes against the velvet and harmonizes with the silk.

3. I then edged the quilt with a double binding of the silk using the method outlined in the Attic Windows bed quilt project (see "Binding the Quilt," page 59.)

Although I had originally designed this keepsake as a lap quilt, I changed my mind when a friend expressed her horror at the prospect of a twelve-year-old using an antique in that way. "Her girlfriends will be sitting on it while they put on nail polish. Somebody will spill it and say, 'Sorry about that.' You want this to last more than five minutes, don't you?" I added a row of silk tabs so that it could be hung on a wall.

Here I had quartered one of three antique squares. Note the blue-and-white fabric just under the embroidered names. It seems oddly modern compared to the other fabrics. The dye is brighter and the contrast stronger. Perhaps it was the last piece Martha added to the collection.

After I had quartered and trimmed all three squares, I arranged them in a balanced pattern. I put the square embroidered with the names of the quilters on the lower right.

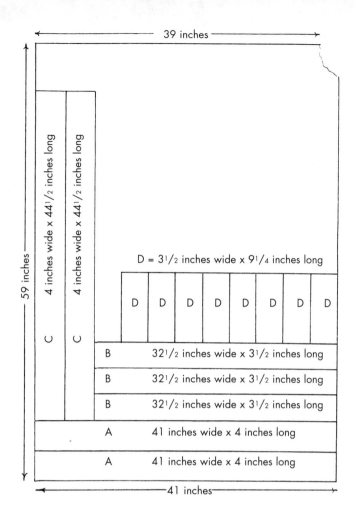

39 inches

59 inches

C — 4 inches wide × 44 1/2 inches long

C — 4 inches wide × 44 1/2 inches long

D = 3 1/2 inches wide × 9 1/4 inches long

| D | D | D | D | D | D | D | D |

B — 32 1/2 inches wide × 3 1/2 inches long

B — 32 1/2 inches wide × 3 1/2 inches long

B — 32 1/2 inches wide × 3 1/2 inches long

A — 41 inches wide × 4 inches long

A — 41 inches wide × 4 inches long

41 inches

I planned a cutting layout for the velvet sashes and borders so that all the nap would run in the same direction on the finished quilt. The pieces marked A are the top and bottom borders; those marked B are the horizontal sashes; those marked C are the side borders; and those marked D are the vertical sashes.

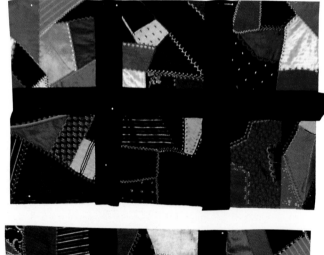

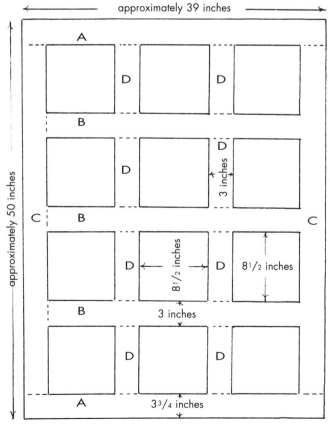

approximately 39 inches

approximately 50 inches

A

D   D

B

D   D

3 inches

C   B   C

D   8 1/2 inches   D   8 1/2 inches

B   3 inches

D   D

A   3 3/4 inches

Here I had sewn one horizontal and six vertical sashes to the squares.

Having a design plan for the lap quilt made assembling the pieces easier.

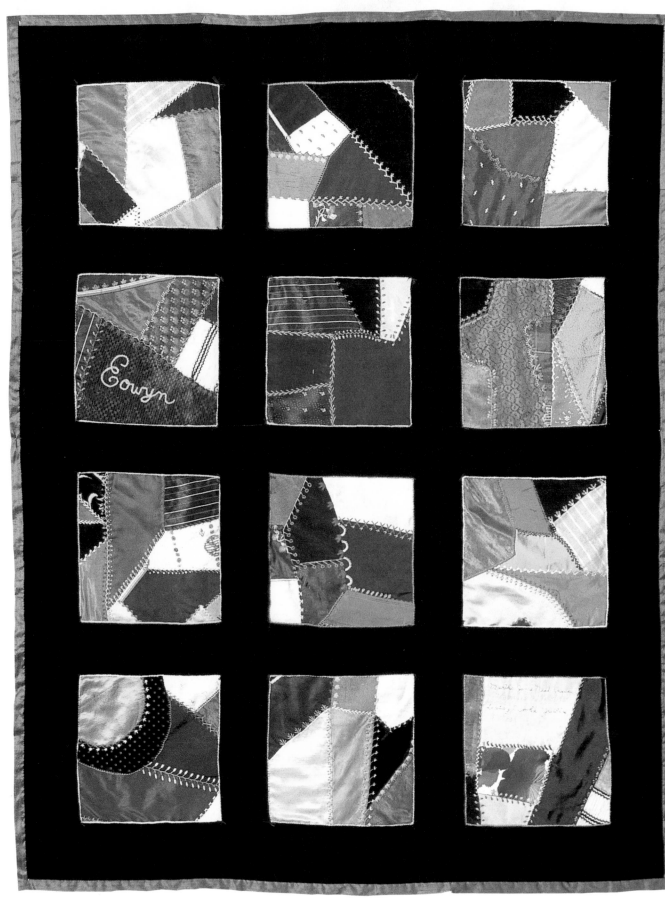

On the finished lap quilt the corners of the binding are butted in the same direction as the border strips. Photo by Breger and Assoc., Inc.

A "FELINE" PILLOW

Jennifer, Martha's great-granddaughter, loves cats. For her I chose a square on which Martha had embroidered the initials of her uncle, Jim Neal, on a bit of pale lavender ribbon and embellished it with flowers.

Embellishing and Repairing the Square

1. I appliquéd tiny cats in several colors as well as a larger black-and-white cat. Embroidering yellow eyes, a pink nose, and a hint of a red tongue on the latter created a striking sense of three-dimensionality. I embroidered the edges of all cats and seams and added Jennifer's initials (J.W.) in a flourishing chain stitch across two velvet patches at the top above a matching cat.

2. A piece of green and black silk on the lower left had shredded with age. I covered it with burgundy lace to hold it in place, creating a lively effect where the color underneath shows through. In the days when that silk was made it was sold by the pound, so manufacturers would impregnate it with mineral salts to make it heavier. Over time, however, the mineral salts caused the silk to deteriorate. Perhaps that was the case with this piece. The antique quilt shown on page 99 is disintegrating because of the presence of mineral salts.

Completing the Pillow

I used welt cord covered with black velvet to finish and stiffen the edges of this square. I attached backing in the same fabric, slipped an 18-inch pillow form inside, and sewed it shut. As this pillow cover is not washable, no opening was needed.

Eleven squares remain to be used as the basis for keepsakes for Martha Neal Craven's great-grandson, Douglas, and six more great-great-grandchildren. Many pleasant hours lie ahead.

I used this unembellished square as the base for Jenny's cat pillow.

I distributed the cats over the surface of the square and appliquéd them in place, arranging them so that they would contrast with the background fabrics.

The finished pillow. Photo by Breger and Assoc., Inc.

(Right) GRANDMOTHER'S FLOWER GARDEN
by Blanche Dashner Jelley
and her sisters. 65 × 75 inches.
*This traditional quilt, which was made in
the 1920s, shows the effects of mineral salt
damage. Niece-in-law Ellen Dashner attached
a filmy overlay of crepeline to hold the silk
together. Photo by Breger and Assoc., Inc.*

CHAPTER 8

WEARABLE QUILT ART

he creative process is its own reward, but the effect that the work has on others is a part of the process, part of its life. Art is created at least to some extent to affect those who see it, to change or enrich them in some way. This rebounds to the artist, causing still further changes that may affect subsequent creative efforts. Making a quilt that is not confined to the home but can go out into the world as wearable art expands the artist's range. Using a simple garment pattern to express your artistry is also an excellent way to build toward the creative challenges of the original art quilt, which is discussed in the following chapter.

(Opposite) This vest is made of black silk chiffon over peach-colored rayon, which I then crazy-quilted with patches and bands of lace, braid, and ribbon and embellished with beads, buttons, bows, and embroidery.
(Above) The tools of the quilter's craft combine with those of the dressmaker to create wearable art.

Project: A Strip-Pieced Hippari

The front of the silk chiffon vest shown on page 100 is also elaborately decorated.

Wearable art exists outside of fashion trends. It makes a timeless statement. In selecting a pattern for a garment on which to compose a quilted image, simplicity is a primary consideration. Passing fashion is not. You can buy a commercial pattern as a gauge for length, armhole shape, waist size, and other details, then simplify it, or take the applicable measurements from another garment and design something completely new.

In searching for suitable patterns for these demonstrations I ran across a company called Folkwear, Inc. They publish, among others, a pattern for a garment worn by Japanese field workers called a *hippari*, which is cut, as much folkwear is, from one rectangular piece of cloth with virtually no leftover scrap. This constitutes efficient use of handwoven fabric in any society where thrift is a matter of survival. The same efficiency suits the designer of artwear.

MAKING A FABRIC STUDY

1. Select or develop a garment pattern that is composed of one or more nearly rectangular shapes, such as a kimono, poncho, caftan, or possibly a cape. These are well suited to strip piecing.
2. Make a fabric study, using card stock as a base on which to compose a line design. Then cut and paste strips of fabric, rearranging them until you are satisfied with the composition. These strips should vary in width. On the hippari I made for the demonstration they range from a very fine line of pale blue-gray to a broad band of dark print. The design is united by affinities of color, shape, value, and line, the diagonals breaking into what might otherwise be monotonous horizontality. Similar values of the solid colors relate strongly to each other even when widely separated. If you use a light stock you can fold the completed fabric study to see how the pattern will look when worn.

PIECING AND PRESSING

Make your garment full size in unbleached muslin and sew onto it overlapping strips according to the fabric study. Where strips come together from two directions, join them by hand with a slipstitch or blindstitch. The method is similar to that used for the crazy quilt square in Chapter 7 (see page 82). As with a crazy quilt, no batting is necessary because the strips are stitched to a fabric backing.

I added a second, wider pale blue-gray collar band not called for in the original pattern, making a double border for the front of the composition. I also added pockets in the side seams for convenience.

FINISHING THE GARMENT

You might want to consider adding shoulder pads, which help to hold the design up to view. For the lining of the hippari I used the same pale blue-gray as the thinnest strip and the second collar band. To fasten the garment in the front, I made two ties from the dark blue solid fabric, which I finished at the ends with a traditional knot.

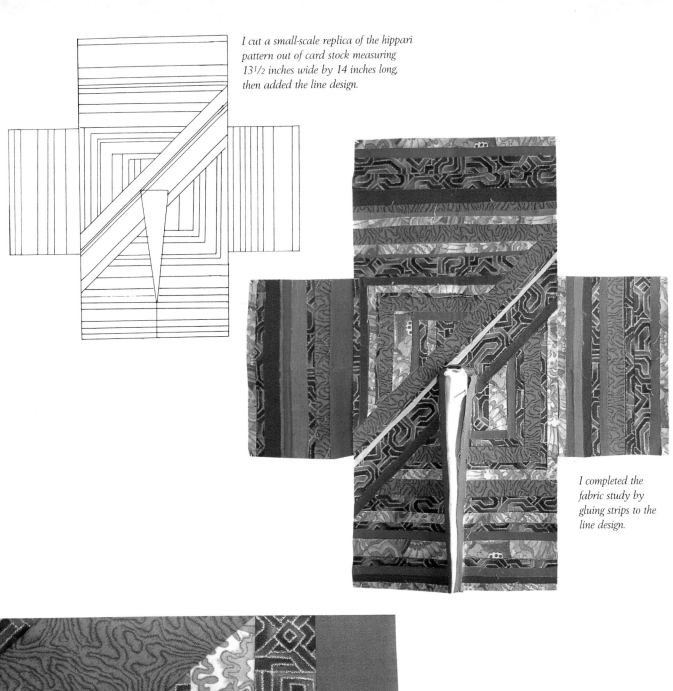

I cut a small-scale replica of the hippari pattern out of card stock measuring 13½ inches wide by 14 inches long, then added the line design.

I completed the fabric study by gluing strips to the line design.

I made a plain muslin hippari first to use as the base for strip piecing.

Both the front and the back of the finished garment display variety of hue, linear direction, print pattern, and width of stripes.

Project: A "Holly and Ivy" Holiday Vest

On the spur of the moment, when there were many holiday parties to go to and I wanted something different to wear, I made a quilted vest. There was no time to make a fabric study, little time to plan the layout, and less time to shop for fabrics. I had just enough solid primary red left over from the backing that I used for the Attic Windows bed quilt (see page 59) to cut a simple vest from a McCall's pattern (#6786) and to piece a lining from its last scraps. I happened to have on hand a piece of ultra-thin batting that I had originally purchased for the "Constellations" quilt in the memorial triptych (see page 125). Because it was thinner than the batting I had used in the other two quilts, I put it away for a rainy day (but used it on a snowy one instead).

MAKING THE VEST

Choose any vest pattern and make it fully lined. Your finished vest is the canvas on which you compose your design.

When I completed the one I made for the demonstration, I tried it on and found that there was no need for the ties used to pull in the waist at the back. (These would have interfered with the appliqué anyway.) Shocking to behold—there wasn't even sufficient crossover in the front for buttonholes! Had I gained that much weight already, with the holiday season only half over? The solution was to sew on small hemispheric gold buttons close to the edge of the left front and insert into the edge seam on the right loops of gold elastic salvaged from a wrapped gift.

DEVELOPING AND APPLIQUÉING THE DESIGN

1. Choose some classic appliqué patterns, or design your own. Cut them out of paper to see how they can be arranged on your vest. For this demonstration I decided to make a design of holly and ivy: a holly tree on the back of the vest with ivy starting at its base and twining around the hem and up the front. I went out in the snow and cut a small branch of holly and another of ivy. I photocopied them each several

times, cut out the prints, and, twisting the paper stems, laid them out in various arrangements on the vest. Using natural materials in this way could provide components for unlimited design possibilities.

2. Select fabrics and cut shapes using your paper patterns. I went through my collection of green and turquoise fabrics to find six for holly leaves and a different set of seven for ivy. These included several shades of solid green, some tiny black-on-green prints, some moderate-size patterns that included other colors, and some fine stripes. Many of these textiles had gold metallic elements. Only one, which depicted holly leaves and berries, could be considered a "Christmas" print.

3. Try various ways of arranging your cutouts on your vest. I accumulated a pile of fabric leaves to play with in working out my image. When I was satisfied with the layout I applied each holly leaf using green thread and a straight stitch.

4. You can use almost any appliqué method described in Chapter 6 to mount your composition on your vest. In the demonstration project I covered the edge of each holly leaf with a satin stitch using kelly green bobbin thread

and green metallic top thread. (This is the technique described for the African print banner in Chapter 6, page 74, and for the "Balloons" crib quilt in Chapter 9, page 113.)

5. Using a blue water-erasable fabric marker, I drew branches connecting the holly leaves, then covered these lines also with green metallic satin stitch. (You could use heavy embroidery floss, cording, braid, or strings of sequins for different effects.)

6. Next I worked on the ivy leaves and stems, changing the top thread for the satin stitch to red metallic while continuing with the kelly green bobbin. The green metallic thread had worked very smoothly on my Kenmore machine. Fortunately this was the color I used first. If I had first used the red, which broke every couple of inches, I would have completely given up on the idea of using metallic thread. (I returned the spool of red to the store, and the manager gave me a new one that worked fine. I still don't know what was wrong with the first one.) Because the bobbin thread was green for both the holly and the ivy, the inside of the vest displays a green line drawing of the outside design. You can see in the photo at the bottom of the opposite page that on some leaves I stitched the lines of the veins.

MAKING REVISIONS

When you have finished your appliqué, put it away for a day or so, then look at it again with fresh eyes to consider possible modifications. When my vest was finished I tried it on and was disappointed because it wasn't as striking as I had expected it to be. The problem was that there was not enough contrast of value. The solution was easy. I chose another print in a light-value green for the ivy and a different light green for the holly, and used them for a few small leaves here and there. The effect was just what I wanted.

A pair of cream-colored slacks and a cream-colored blouse provided a background against which to present this festive work of art.

I photocopied some real holly leaves, cut them out, and pinned them on the vest.

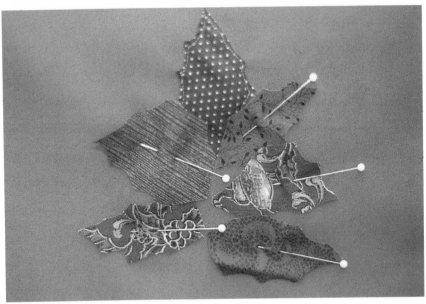

I then replaced the paper holly leaves with fabric ones.

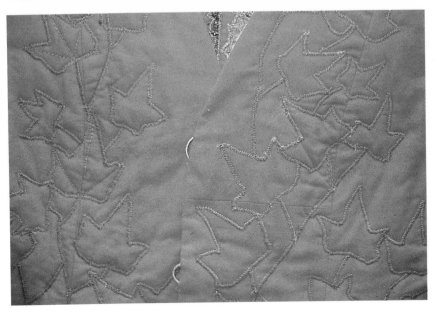

Inside the vest the green bobbin thread traces the design against the red lining.

The back of the finished vest (above) shows the holly tree, while the front (opposite) adds the sparkle of gold buttons to the appliquéd design of twining ivy.

CHAPTER 9

ORIGINAL DESIGNS: THE ART QUILT

A work of art has a life of its own after it leaves the hands of the artist, acting as both a vehicle of expression and a catalyst of emotion and memory. A quilt can play a part in developing a child's sense of place, as in "The Pedricks at Home," which features a landscape that simultaneously reflects photographic sources and the whim of recollection. A quilt can also become a part of a larger community and include an ongoing development of design, as in the memorial quilts on which new names are embroidered as old friends depart. It can even be a part of the history of a family and a nation, as is Julia Amelia Hauser's quilt, "Peony I" (see page 9), in which the family silver was hidden during Sherman's march. In this chapter we survey three examples of the original art quilt, the melding of a quilter's singular vision and traditional piecing and quilting techniques.

(Opposite) MEET ME IN ST. LOUIS *by Christine Adams.*
This example of free-motion quilting with metallics and netting uses
a repetitive fish motif to create an original design. Photo by Ronnie Haber.
(Above) Some designing tools and several collections of simple objects,
which might inspire a composition.

Project: A "Balloons" Crib Quilt

I wanted to make a crib quilt for a friend who was about to have a baby. The simplest shape that came to mind as evocative of childhood was a balloon.

In my mind's eye the picture was at first only a cluster of overlapping circles. This narrowed the problem down to one of color, so in "Balloons" the dominant contrast is that of hue. Although it would have been possible to suggest the volume of the balloons through gradations of value I decided for simplicity's sake to use a flat representation. This gives the image a crisp, modern look.

PLANNING THE DESIGN

1. I began by calling a mail order company that carries crib quilts to find out their dimensions. The answer, 41 by 32 inches, is small enough that by taping four large sheets of newsprint together I could draw a full-size replica.

2. My design required templates, which I drew in three sizes and a range of shapes. I had started out by repeating a single shape, a circle, but as the plan developed I included ovals and pear shapes as well. With the templates I drew a cluster of overlapping balloons on the big paper rectangle, then used my T-square to add strings leading to a single point near the bottom.

3. Instead of making a full-size fabric

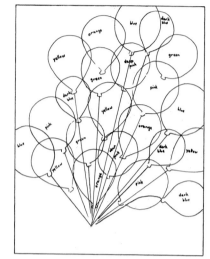

The layout drawing in pencil shows three repeated shapes in various sizes.

The tissue paper study has each color widely scattered.

On the full-size quilt top, here pinned to show preliminary placement, note the small bit of a red balloon in the center.

COLOR NOTE

"MIXING" FABRIC COLORS

Small children usually prefer primary colors because they offer the most vigorous and the clearest identity of hue. As we discussed in Chapter 2, red and yellow make orange, red and blue make violet, and yellow and blue make green. These secondary colors are a little less vivid and offer less contrast than the primaries. For variety, the "Balloons" quilt includes both of the above classifications of hue. The challenge was to arrange them in an interesting manner.

study, I cut balloon shapes from colored tissue paper and pinned them over the drawing. I distributed three large blue balloons over the area of the design, then three large pinks, followed by a large yellow just above the center point, which I planned to embroider later with the baby's name and birth date. I then fanned out three more large yellows across the face of the quilt and filled the areas between with overlapping smaller balloons whose hues increased in intensity as they diminished in size. Some colors predominate and others appear only in a few small patches.

ESTIMATING YARDAGE

Since none of the balloons was larger than 9 inches in its smaller dimension, a $1/4$ yard of each color was plenty. The sky and grass each required $2/3$ yard. The backing and binding used most of $1 1/2$ yards.

APPLIQUÉING THE TOP

1. While putting together the fabric top, I decided to add a tiny piece of pure red as a portion of one of the balloons. Its color was so hot and so saturated that it attracted attention out of proportion to its size, which is why it's small and near the center of the quilt. I cut whole balloons from solid color fabrics and moved them around on the layout, playing with various arrangements, their overlapping edges modifying the colors. As I had done in the paper sketch, I distributed the hues and values more or less evenly over the quilt. This creates an active pattern, as the colors and shapes bounce to and fro across the composition.

2. It occurred to me that it might be more interesting to introduce print fabrics by exposing a bit of background as sky and grass. I then began to think of putting strings on the balloons. My first idea was to drape them all together, bunching them in a loose knot, which led to the thought of including a baby's hand holding them. I sketched and cut out a paper hand to use as a pattern for a fabric one. The placement seemed static, so I moved the baby's hand to the lower left corner, reorienting all the balloons in the process. I pinned a ribbon running from each balloon to the hand, establishing the direction of movement. The ribbon strings wrap around the hand and arm, then fly off to the right as if blown by the same breeze that pushes the balloons.

Sky and grass add texture to the composition. Ribbons add movement and provide quilting lines in the expanse of grass.

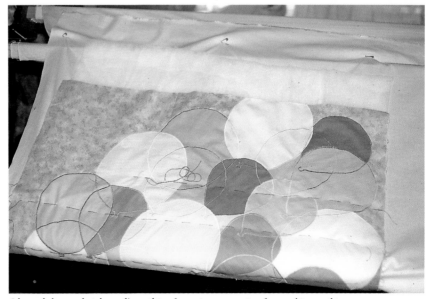

I basted the sandwich on the quilting frame in preparation for machine quilting.

3. Once the layout was set, I top-stitched the pieces together ⅛ inch inside the edges. Where light colors overlapped dark ones, the fabric beneath showed through just enough to make a shadow and modify the hue of the top one. Where three layers overlapped, I trimmed away the bottom one to reduce thickness and to keep the shifts in color clear and distinct.

4. Pressing this quilt top was a delicate job because there were so many bias edges. The straight of the goods should be parallel to the sides of the quilt, but all the shapes are curved and I had moved them around while developing the composition. The bias seldom ended up where it had started.

BASTING AND QUILTING THE SANDWICH

I chose a yellow fabric for the backing and binding because I didn't know yet whether the baby would be a girl or a boy. Following the procedures described in Chapter 3, I sandwiched a low-loft polyester batting (the same used in the Attic Windows bed quilt, page 57) between the top and the backing.

1. I fastened the lower edge of the sandwich to the front bar of my three-bar quilting frame and draped the rest across the back. I basted the sandwich from side to side about every 5 inches using black thread so that it would show up clearly. The basting stitches were rather short to minimize their catching on the presser foot.

2. I removed the quilt from the frame and, using thread in colors that matched each balloon, I quilted the sandwich with a machine satin-stitch over the top-stitching lines. This delineated the shapes, emphasizing the direction in which they were tilted.

EMBELLISHMENTS

I filled the two biggest unquilted areas with the embroidered text of the baby's name and birth date, which I added after he was born. The ribbons I used for the balloon strings provided lines for quilting over the grass area. I included one red ribbon to brighten up that part of the quilt, but it overbalanced the composition. Covering some of it with other paler ribbons failed to solve the problem completely. It seemed to me that something red but very small was needed in the upper left area, where I also needed quilting lines. The most obvious solution was a tiny red kite high in the sky. The kite, with its string and its tail, provided the quilting lines, gave a feeling of depth to the composition, and was the perfect balance for the reds.

BINDING THE QUILT

For the binding I used a double straight-grain fabric, the same one I used for the backing. I sewed it using the method described for the One-Patch quilt (see Chapter 3, "Binding the Quilt," page 41), except that the corners are mitered.

Shown opposite and on page 110 are two other examples—one done in a traditional manner, the other in a contemporary style—of how the repeated forms of common objects can make appealing compositions.

(Above) I added a red kite in the upper left corner to balance the distribution of red and to provide quilting lines in the sky. The quilt is bound with mitered corners. Photo by Breger and Assoc., Inc.

(Right) When the baby was born, I added his name and birthdate to the finished quilt.

114

BUTTERFLIES by Nancy Shapiro. 1992.
In this pattern, which the quilter dates from the 1940s, the simple shape of a butterfly has been stylized and divided into smaller shapes.

Project: A Queen-Size Bed Quilt

The way that my daughter Carolyn's house nestles into the Vermont landscape inspired the subject of this bed quilt. In this demonstration, we will focus on the part that line plays in setting up the rhythms and directions of movement.

DEVELOPING THE IMAGE

When the idea for "The Pedricks At Home" was germinating, I took some photos of the property in order to settle in my mind which elements I wanted to include. These boiled down to: the family (including the two dogs), the house, the pole barn, the swings, the vegetable garden, the orchard, the trees lining the driveway, the mail boxes, the girls' hideaway up in the woods and the path leading to it, and the trees and flowerbeds near the house. In reality these would not all be visible from one point of view so I had to bend physical reality to the needs of emotional reality. This bending process began with the sketch and was continued by the color study.

When gathering data to use for designing "The Pedricks at Home," I collected photographs of my daughter's family and the Vermont landscape as well as pictures cut from magazines.

A rough sketch includes the main features of the quilt.

COLOR NOTE

"TRYING ON" ANOTHER PALETTE

This composition is intended to portray summer in Vermont. In studying the few color photographs I had of Carolyn's home, I saw that some of the fields had a yellow cast. the lawn area included a variety of greens. There were dark wooded places, sunny distant valleys, and the far mountains in muted darker colors. I wanted to take into account my daughter's favorite colors, which included emerald and forest green, blue-reds, and the palest shades of every hue but peach, eliminating orange. This is not a palette that comes naturally to me, but it was fun to discipline myself to a different range. The colors around us affect us emotionally, so it makes sense to live among those that please us most.

The oil pastel suggests contrasts of value and modifies the composition.

On this quilt I directed attention to the house by using a range of linear devices, including converging lines, which are rudimentary in the first rough sketch. They are developed and refined in the oil pastel, in which I simplified the forms, reworked the placement of various features, and removed much of the left foreground bank of trees in order to broaden the field and increase the sense of a swelling hillside. The driveway leads the eye from the lower left between the fields up to the house, and the rail fences also taper in that direction. It was easier to simplify the enlarged line drawing because the problems of color were eliminated. The distant hills point like arrows at the house. The fabric study adds dark value and saturated hue to the hills, reinforcing the energy of that movement.

The clouds embrace the house from above, and the dark band of the highest sky frames the picture, keeping our eyes from straying out of the scene. Remembering that the most exciting part of a composition occurs where the darkest dark meets the lightest light, I set the house with its dark roof against the lightest blue of the sky. The fact that blue recedes reinforces the dominance of the house.

The piecing accentuates the serenity of the sky through horizontal lines, conveying a feeling of restfulness. Slow and stately, vertical lines lift, plunge, extend, and direct attention upward. Diagonals give a feeling of movement, activity, and greater speed than horizontal or vertical elements. The contours of the land are defined by the edges of the patches. The quilting echoes the directional forces of the patchwork. This is done through the "stitch-in-the-ditch" and the other quilting lines that run through the fields, funneling toward the house or along the contours of the hills and valleys. The effect is made more explicit by the use of contrasting color threads. The flow of many of these lines toward the house evokes the feeling of coziness which was the scene's original appeal.

I arranged the Pedrick family on this quilt so that the relationship of its members to each other is reinforced by the shape of the land. I placed the figures along an arc that cradles the house. The quilting of the trees draws attention to the swelling growth of the foliage and the upward thrust of their trunks. The relationships of repeated forms imply line, movement, direction,

Over the oil pastel a sheet of tracing paper carries a grid for enlarging the image.

A slightly enlarged drawing focuses on linear design.

117

and even speed. The trees along the drive diminish in height as they recede from the foreground. The sizes of the patches forming the fields also grow smaller as they approach the house, appearing to gather speed. The quilting lines that follow the contour of the land induce an almost giddy sensation as they plunge downslope toward the driveway.

MAKING THE FABRIC STUDY

I began a fabric study with pieces from my collection. I wanted to have as complete an idea as possible of what more I would have to buy, so that one trip around the local fabric shops would take care of most needs. Of course, as the work developed, unexpected problems arose, calling for a still wider selection. In designing a traditional patchwork quilt, it is possible to calculate ahead of time exactly how much yardage of each value and hue is required and be fairly confident of obtaining suitable materials all at once. When you use fabric as a sort of paint-

ing medium, the extent of the palette required is not so precise.

I describe this process in detail below so that you can see that a work of art grows and develops over time. It doesn't simply spring to life in perfect and final form—at least, not for me. Note that it's generally not a good idea to work on one part of a design until it seems finished before going on to the others. Each part affects the rest, causing the need for further changes throughout.

Use your imagination in adapting prints to specific purposes. For example, I modified a print of pieces of jewelry for the rock outcropping near the house, cutting between the colored gems and using only the silver parts of the print.

1. On the first go-round I started laying out the sky with the darkest blue of Carolyn's colors at the top. I proceeded with roughly equal strips of lighter and lighter shades. But I reached the horizon with blues that were still too dark. This is not a night scene, so I started

over again at the horizon with my lightest blue, adding three new values and making the strips narrower. That was better but not good enough.

2. At last it dawned on me that the pale blues near the horizon had to be wider, with each stripe decreasing in width until the final blue at the top was very narrow but still served as a frame to stop the eye from wandering off the edge of the composition.

3. As I applied fresh strips I realized that there weren't enough middle tones. The dark upper sky occupied too much space, and there was an abrupt horizontal line where the darks met the lights. After shopping for more medium blues it was an easy job to pull the pasted strips off the panel, trim them to make them narrower, and then paste on the greater range of values from deep to light blue. The effect was a smoother transition from dark to light, but the real answer to the problem at last became apparent. A number of the darkest blues had to be completely eliminated, letting the middle tones serve as darks. This brightened the daylight considerably and still allowed the top edge of the quilt to serve as a relatively dark stop.

4. It seemed as if the effect would be enhanced by using curved bands instead of straight stripes. Time and effort were well spent pulling off some of the sky fabric again and recutting it. All of this was accomplished at negligible cost. If I had conducted these experiments on the full sized quilt, it would have been expensive and much more time consuming.

5. I began gluing fabric to the fields in the foreground without a precise plan for the shape of each piece, concerned primarily with highlighting the crest of a rise and using less intense illumination in the hollows. The line drawing was 80 percent covered before I ran out of appropriate swatches. Later I recut each piece to take into account linear direction, making the lines running more or less left to right, follow the contours of the land to reinforce the sensation of rolling hills. Lines running roughly up and down were altered to point toward the house, accentuating its importance in the composition. In the process I refined the distribution of light and dark values to further emphasize the curvature of the land. I made a serious search of my fabric collection to find more pieces that could be included both to enlarge the array of patterns

The fabric study reveals flaws in value relationships.

Part of the full-size drawing spread out on the studio floor illustrates the change in scale from fabric study to queen-size quilt.

and to increase the number of grada-tions from dark to light, enhancing the effect of contour. Frequently where a certain value was missing the reverse side of a fabric provided exactly what was needed.

6. I took the incomplete study with me to G Street Fabrics where I knew I would find the widest possible range of choices. This is best done at an hour when the shop is likely to be less busy. The staff members are enthusias-tic about helping with the search for the perfect fabric. With the study spread out on the counter it was easy to see whether the colors and tones on a bolt of cloth were precisely what I was looking for.

7. Back at the drawing board with the new, freshly washed and pressed materi-als, I found that each addition altered the relationships of value and hue. When I backed off to look at the com-position from a distance, it became obvious that the stacked wood was far too dark. When the field on the left was lightened and tonal gradations modified, the row of trees by the lower driveway also appeared too dark. Lucki-ly I had bought a beautifully patterned medium green for these trees. The veg-etable garden was too dark and seemed

like a hole in the picture. The stone wall in the upper right was too dark and so were the rocks in the garden in front of the garage. I had known the dis-tant mountains needed to be lighter and had bought a slightly paler turquoise to replace the deep indigo temporarily occupying that place. The turquoise lit up the whole area, its slightly greener hue making a more live-ly contrast with the sky. The stretch of red flowers in the foreground was too bright and had to be replaced with a darker print.

SCALING UP

1. I placed a grid drawn on tracing paper over the fabric study and used this to enlarge the design to full size. The squares on my fabric study were 3 1/4 inches, and those on the full size pattern were 12-inch blocks on large sheets of newsprint taped together and spread out on the floor of the studio. I used a set of French curves and some jar lids to develop the shapes of the clouds.

2. Over this layout I rolled tracing paper, traced the line design, labeled each piece, and made slash marks across the edges of each piece to identify how they fit together. This was also helpful

later in determining whether the trac-ing paper pattern was right side up.

CUTTING, PIECING, AND PRESSING

It's easier to handle large, complex pro-jects like this when you approach them as a series of small problems. This made the piecing part of the process less over-whelming.

I tried to keep the straight grain of the fabric parallel to the sides of the quilt, but couldn't be rigid about this. Sometimes a print pattern served a design purpose better on the bias. There were so many curving seams that, just as with the "Balloons" crib quilt, I had to be careful while pressing not to stretch the bias.

1. I cut out a few pieces of the paper pattern, adding a 1/4-inch seam allowance around it, and cut freshly pressed fabric.

2. I set one piece at the top of the sky on the full-size line drawing on the floor, and over that fit the next lower piece in the design, matching seam lines and slash marks. I stitched these two together on the seam line, pressed the seam, then satin-stitched over it. I dis-covered that a 1/4-inch seam allowance was too much because the top raw edge

showed beside the satin stitch. From then on I cut the fabrics so that the pieces that would lie on top of a seam had only an 1/8-inch seam allowance, and the ones beneath a 1/2 inch or more, which I later trimmed, so there was leeway for adjustment. I pressed the work after adding each piece to be sure that everything was lying flat.

3. As I continued to work I modified the design at every stage. Sometimes I changed the shape of a pattern simply because I wanted to use a small scrap of an additional fabric. After piecing the whole sky, I spread it out on the full-size drawing to be sure it was still the right size and shape. Here precision was not important (this is a very forgiving method of appliqué) so this was a good point at which to refine the technique. I found a much more beautiful pale blue print as a substitute for a solid that I had used in the clouds. Carefully cutting along the outside of the seams, I removed the offending pieces and replaced them with the new ones, which had to be cut slightly larger.

4. Next I pieced the area of the house, trees, mountains, and background fields, then added this whole section to the sky. I redesigned the little copse in the upper right just before cutting the pieces to create a more interesting group of shapes. I was careful to use medium values rather than dark ones next to the sky so that the contrast would be less striking and not detract attention from the house.

5. The next section was composed of the yellow fields on the right with the vegetable garden, the pole barn, and its shadow. Then I pieced the yellow fields on the left with the row of trees at the edge, followed by the green fields and driveway, and finally the dark vegetation along the bottom and lower sides.

6. When I was ready to begin working on the woodland section on the right, I lined up all my possible fabric choices and rearranged them once more in the sequence they would occupy on the quilt. The trunks of the trees stood out against a paler green understory, but that didn't make sense—it should be

dark there. Another rule of thumb is that while you shouldn't change values within deep shadows, changing hues is fine. With this in mind, I put a darker green between the tree trunks. Suddenly that part of the composition looked right. Because they were narrow, I sewed the tree trunks on top of a piece of background vegetation, then trimmed it away from behind them. The moose is camouflaged both by the darkness of the fabric and by quilting lines, which distract from his form. I superimposed the human figures after the whole composition was assembled. I made the fences from narrow ribbon—an intense blue in the foreground and a gray-blue for the distant ones—and added them along with the quilting.

QUILTING THE SANDWICH

1. I quilted this coverlet with "stitch-in-the-ditch" over the entire area to stabilize the whole sandwich. Removing the third rail from the frame so that the quilt could roll back and forth between the front and back rails, I began the fun of adding the ribbon fences. I quilted the fan on the house siding, the fruit on the solid green tree, and filled all large unquilted areas with new patterns. I had made the mindless decision to outline Megan, the darker dog, in dark blue thread, which made her appear as as a dark hole in the lawn. So in the middle of quilting I had to pick out the satin stitch and replace it with hand stitching in pale green. This small job must have taken a couple of hours, but it had to be done. Now Megan rests comfortably on the grass instead of falling through it.

2. When I trimmed the quilt square, the left tree trunk, an important element of the design, was lost. I had to take out quilting threads back to where I could insert a new trunk, which echoes those in the opposite corner, bracketing the scene between.

BACKING AND BINDING

The backing and double binding are a dark blue, which harmonizes with the colors of the top and won't show the dirt, an important consideration for such a busy and active family.

"The Pedricks at Home" represents a whole family and its environment. In her remarkable portraits, one of which appears on page 122, Dorothy Holden concentrates on a single individual, evoking a sense of personality as vividly with fabric as could be done with paint.

I used several needles at once for quilting.

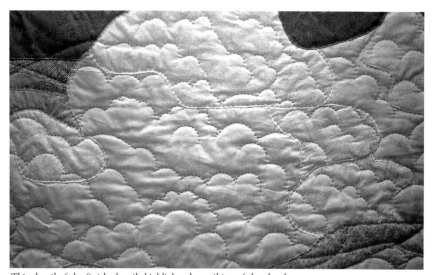

This detail of the finished quilt highlights the quilting of the clouds.

The finished quilt. Photo by Breger and Assoc., Inc.

THE BLUE MOON ANIMAL PARADE
by Dorothy Holden.
Another of Dorothy's original quilt designs,
this one a whimsical appliquéd composition.
Photo by Joseph E. Garland.

MATTHEW
by Dorothy Holden. 17 × 21 inches.
Simple forms combine to trace the bone
structure and posture of a singular man.
Photo by Joseph E. Garland.

122

Project: A Memorial Quilt Triptych

These three quilts began as a memorial to my son, Charles, but they grew to be more than that. They now include individuals from fifty-nine other families of our church and offer themselves as objects for contemplation to all who attend services.

As a quilting project, this demonstration is devoted more to problems of design than to those of construction. I designed the panels to be hung in a new sanctuary on a 28-foot-wide wall behind the pulpit. The width of the wall, which then existed only on architectural drawings, determined the size of the quilts. They had to be large enough so that the image of each would be clear from a distance but small enough to allow breathing room between them. The finished dimensions of each are 63 inches wide by 81 inches high.

UNIFYING ELEMENTS

Their identical size and shape, and their dominant color, blue, draw the quilts together as a triptych. Among them, earth, air, fire, and water are represented. A dark background is a shared characteristic, providing strong contrast with the principal features of each: the flame, the sailboat, both moons, and the lighted side of the earth. Large circular forms echo each other—the flame's aura, the earth, and the radiating light of the moon over the sea—and are accentuated by quilting. Each panel presents an epitaph and a group of names for the viewer's consideration.

Closer examination reveals that the building unit of each quilt is a triangle, as evidenced most dramatically by the two sparks of light against dark blue at the top of "The Flaming Chalice." The red spot at the tip of the wick and the red line below infer a large triangle drawn by the attraction of the reds for each other. The saucer of the chalice is a triangle and the base a smaller inverted one. In "Seascape" the angelfish and the sail and its reflection are triangles. Less obviously in "Constellations," the Milky Way divides the whole quilt roughly into two great triangles.

The red line that traverses "The Flaming Chalice" points to the two flanking panels, as does the rim of the

SEASCAPE
Left panel. 1991. 63 × 81 inches.
Photo by Breger and Assoc., Inc.

chalice. The moon, which is quilted with a smiling face and appears on both side quilts, is accentuated by echo-quilting. The group of eleven women who did the quilting by hand used the paisley shape of the background print on the center panel to make a template. At times we had six around the frame at once. We used the same template on the left-hand panel to quilt the sail and its reflection.

Contrast of Extent

Searching for relief from so much blue in "The Flaming Chalice," your eyes

leap to the red and yellow of the flame and the red line to complete the spectrum. This phenomenon, along with the small extent of red and yellow relative to blue, magnify their importance out of proportion to their size, inviting you to impute meaning to what you see and provoking your intimate interaction with the work. The red line also calls attention away from the center of interest down toward the names.

"Seascape" also offers contrast of proportion between the tiny area of hot orange and the vast blue and turquoise of the sky and sea, setting the mood of

THE FLAMING CHALICE
Center panel. 1990. 63 × 81 inches.
Photo by Breger and Assoc., Inc.

the composition. In "Constellations," the difference in proportion between dark and light makes the earth seem to float in a limitless universe.

Temperature and Intensity
Contrast of extent in each of these compositions is enhanced by cool/warm contrast, as well as that of brilliance. Pure warm yellow and red spring out at us from the grayed blues around the

chalice, the hot orange sailboat shines against the duller sea, and the earth glows warmly in the moonlight against a cold dark sky.

Movement
There is movement in all of these designs. Even the chalice is not static or symmetrical. The wick turns toward its glowing tip, and the flame wavers and blows toward the rising sparks that fly

off, not toward the corner where they would lead your eye out of the picture, but to the right of that, where you could imagine they might ricochet off the edge and head back in another direction within the composition.

One circle of light is higher than the other, and appears to be circulating rapidly around the flame. It is obviously a composition of triangles within squares. The lower circle seems to be

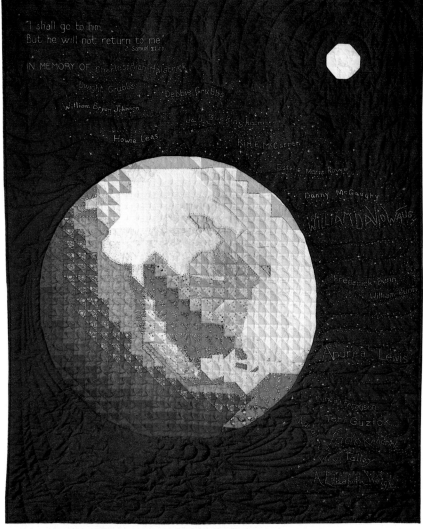

CONSTELLATIONS
Right panel. 1992. 63 × 81 inches.
Photo by Breger and Assoc., Inc.

Three memorial quilts installed in the sanctuary of the Unitarian Universalist Church of Silver Spring, Maryland. Photo by Breger and Assoc., Inc.

more random, a foaming spray of deeper blues filling its allotted space with chaotic abandon. Upon close inspection, you will see that although the personalities of these two circles differ, they are both built on the very same pattern, just as each of us is built on a general human pattern but expresses that humanity in a unique and distinctive way.

In "Seascape," both the patchwork line and the quilted line are prominent factors in the movement of the sea. In the depths, where the names appear, the quilting lines undulate across the seams, creating subtle highlights and shadows that break up the straight parallel bands into wavelike patterns. The edges of the fish form linear rhythms that give character to each school. The angelfish seem to swim toward the center quilt, as do the sharks that exit quickly to the right. Way down below the surface, large gray fish representing the deep subconscious glide slowly toward the left.

In "Constellations," the stars drift through space from the upper left toward the lower right, as though following the earth's rotation.

CONSTRUCTION

All of these quilts take advantage of a special piecing shortcut developed by quilter Barbara Johannah for making

125

two-triangle squares in quantity. This technique, which is referred to in *The Complete Book of Machine Quilting* by Bobbie and Tony Fanning (listed in the Bibliography) is shown at right.

The Flaming Chalice

Each of the overlapping circles within this quilt is composed of two kinds of double-triangle squares, dozens of each kind. I pinned the squares to my fabric wall to be sure they were all turned in the proper directions.

1. Starting at the top, I sewed together each horizontal row of squares, pinning these back in place on the wall as I went. Then I sewed the top row onto the second, and these onto the third, and so on down.

2. When I got to the black wick above the chalice I assembled half rows on either side of it, sewed those on the left to each other, and then those on the right. Finally I joined them all at once to the black wick.

3. The chalice was easy because its strips run in the same direction as the rows of squares. I treated each strip as part of a row of squares.

4. When chalice, flame, and circles were all assembled, I spread them on the background fabric and hand-appliquéd them together. When that was complete, I trimmed away the excess background fabric from behind.

5. The names were embroidered by relatives or friends of those memorialized. For this purpose, I mailed strips of the medium-blue fabric all over the United States and later assembled them as one piece, which I then incorporated in the quilt top.

6. I added the borders by machine except where the image interrupted them. There I appliquéd by hand.

7. As mentioned above, the template for the quilting pattern on most of the top was a simplification of the paisley fabric design. The panel names are quilted stitch-in-the-ditch, and the border with parallel diagonal lines. I finished the panel with a double binding to match the inner border.

Seascape

The sky, moon, and sailboat of "Seascape" were constructed in the same way as the circles and flame of the central quilt. The surface of the sea was sewn together in strips and assembled row by row, as were most of the fish. The angelfish, however, are composed of triangles that cross four rows—

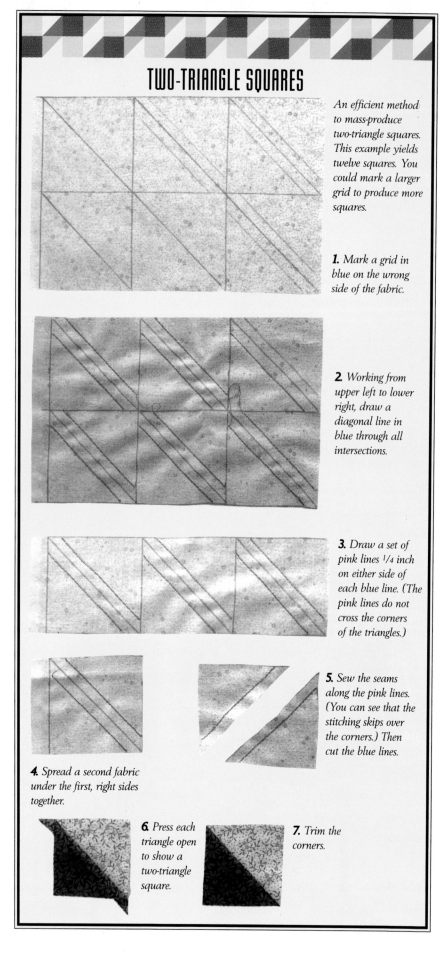

TWO-TRIANGLE SQUARES

An efficient method to mass-produce two-triangle squares. This example yields twelve squares. You could mark a larger grid to produce more squares.

1. *Mark a grid in blue on the wrong side of the fabric.*

2. *Working from upper left to lower right, draw a diagonal line in blue through all intersections.*

3. *Draw a set of pink lines 1/4 inch on either side of each blue line. (The pink lines do not cross the corners of the triangles.)*

5. *Sew the seams along the pink lines. (You can see that the stitching skips over the corners.) Then cut the blue lines.*

4. *Spread a second fabric under the first, right sides together.*

6. *Press each triangle open to show a two-triangle square.*

7. *Trim the corners.*

This detail of "Seascape" shows the variety of styles of embroidery and the personal symbols beside some of the names.

The back of "Constellations" shows the quilting patterns: flowers for the land, waves for water, and stars for the sky. Photo by Breger and Assoc., Inc.

and not always the same four. I handled them in the same way as the black wick above the chalice.

As I had done for the previous quilt, I sent strips of fabric to friends and relatives who did the needlework. You can see a variety of personal touches as people entered into the spirit of the thing.

The quilters had the most fun with this quilt. You can see a school of tiny quilted minnows just below the sharks, a jellyfish done in silver thread below and to the right of the sail's reflection. There is the man in the moon and his winking reflection. Providing a feminine presence, the constellation of the Seven Sisters hovers in the dark sky, six silver stars and one, which in the real sky cannot be seen without a telescope, done in blue. There are many other creatures that invite a closer study of the work. This quilt has no border, only a double binding in one of the sky's darkest blues.

Constellations

"Constellations" is dedicated to the memory of deceased sons and daughters of members of the congregation. I assembled the earth and the moon by the two-triangle square method shown on the opposite page, then hand-appliquéd them on the background fabric. I embroidered the Milky Way in pale blues and yellows in a diagonal swath across the sky, leaving spaces for names. The names, which were stitched only in white, are all done in cross-stitch as though each one were a constellation. These were done by family members or friends who had to borrow the whole quilt top to do the embroidery.

I adapted the design of the earth from a satellite photo, outlining the geographic features with some of the embroidery stitches shown in Chapter 7 (see pages 88 and 89). For the binding I used the same blue as the sky so that it would not impose a limit on the composition.

HANGING METHOD

I hung the triptych according to a method recommended by the Textile Museum in Washington, D.C., that makes it easy to put the quilts up and take them down. I fastened to the wall a piece of lath to which a strip of the hook side of Velcro had been stapled. Along the back of the top edge of the quilt I basted a band of cotton fabric with the soft side of Velcro sewn to it.

PATTERNS FOR TRADITIONAL PIECED QUILTS

For the patterns included in this section, seam allowances are shown as a white band within a black line. Fabric covers the part that will be visible in the finished square. A black-and-white diagram indicates which segments are assembled first, then joined to make a full square or unit. Some hints for the most effective presentation of these patterns can be found on pages 12–13.

COSMIC TRIANGLES by Lois Smith. 1993. 54 × 54 inches.
This is one of a series of quilts designed to explore the possibilities of the triangle. Photo by Breger and Assoc., Inc.

Because of the curved edges of its "petals," this pattern lends itself to the use of a pressing form, over which the seam allowance is folded and pressed. Using the seam lines of the templates as patterns, make pressing forms of light card stock. Steam press the fabric seam allowance over the edges of the pressing forms. Appliqué the assembled plate onto a 14½-inch square of fabric.

Grandmother's Fan

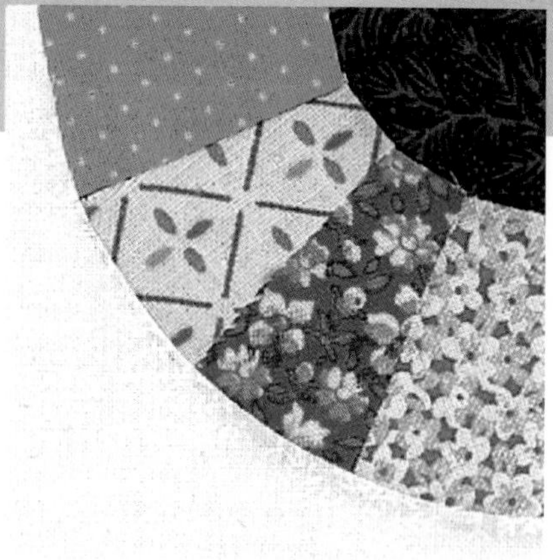

Makes a 7-inch block

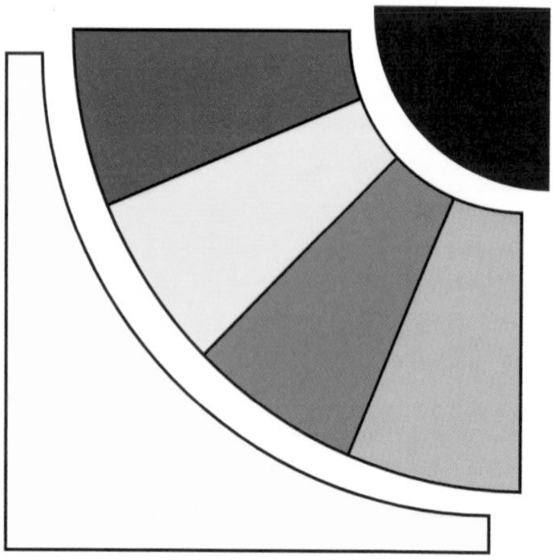

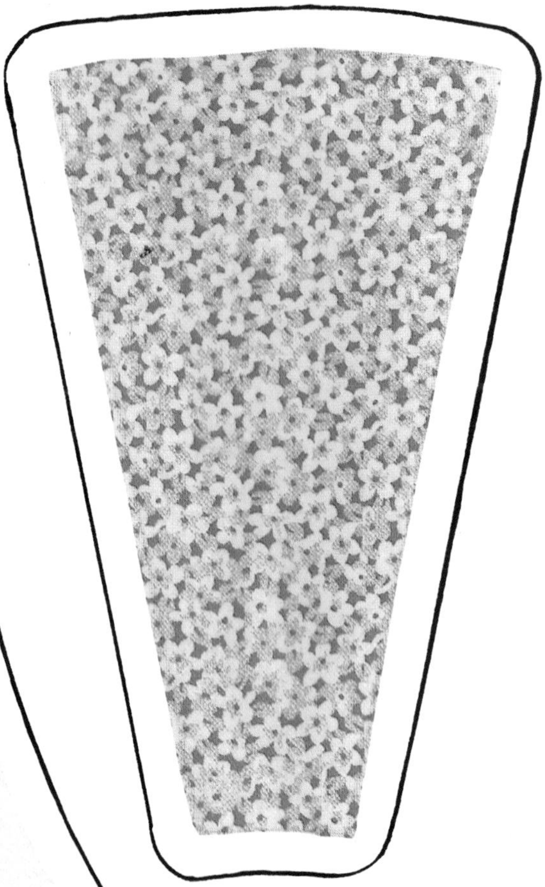

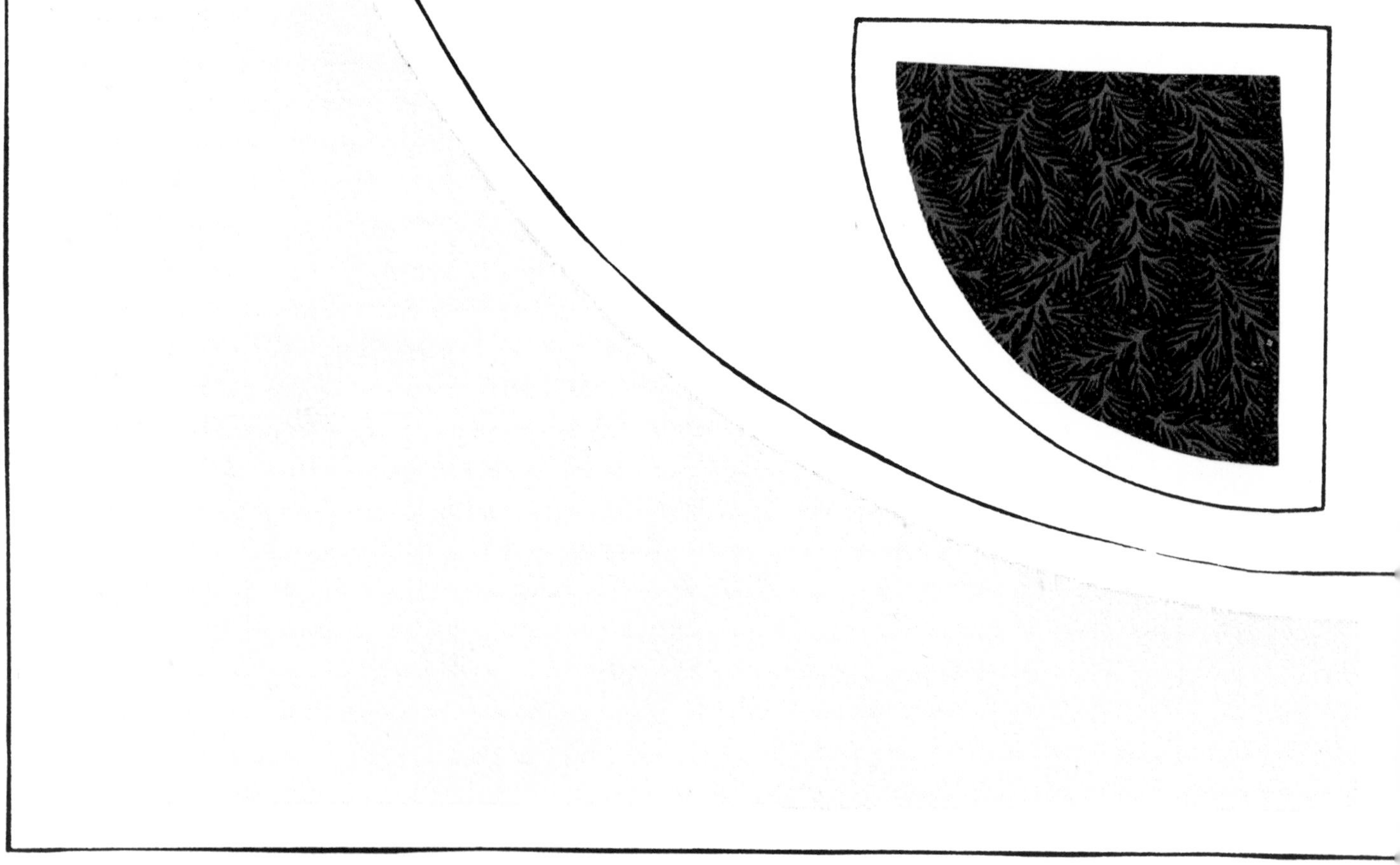

130

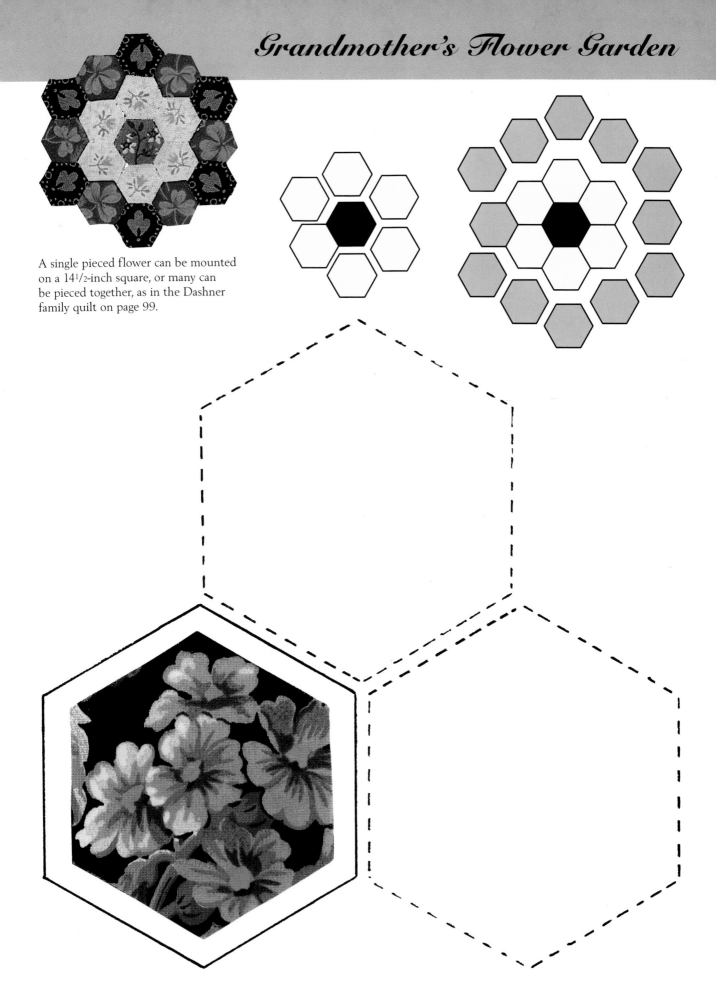

A single pieced flower can be mounted on a 14½-inch square, or many can be pieced together, as in the Dashner family quilt on page 99.

Each block of three patches measures 2¼ inches on a side. You can enlarge or reduce the template below as desired.

Makes a 6-inch block

Makes a 12-inch block

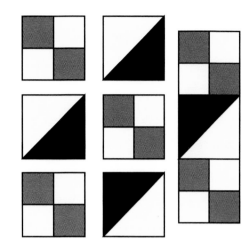

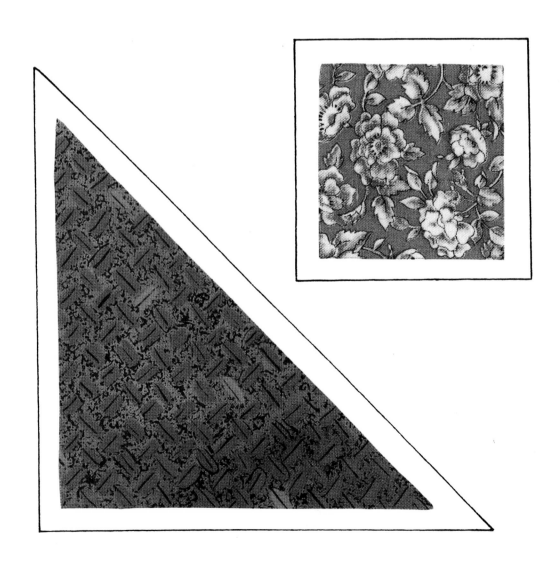

Monkey Wrench

Makes a 12-inch block

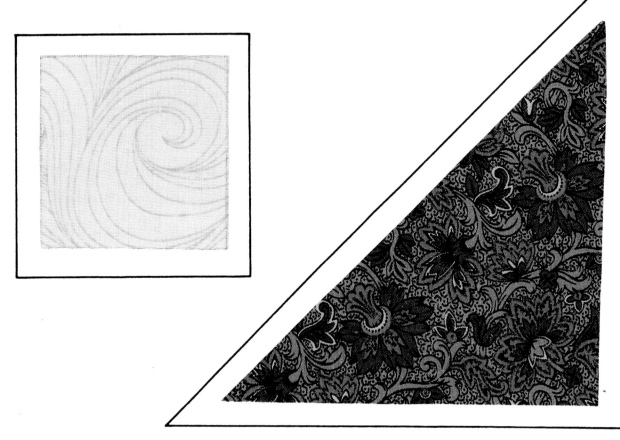

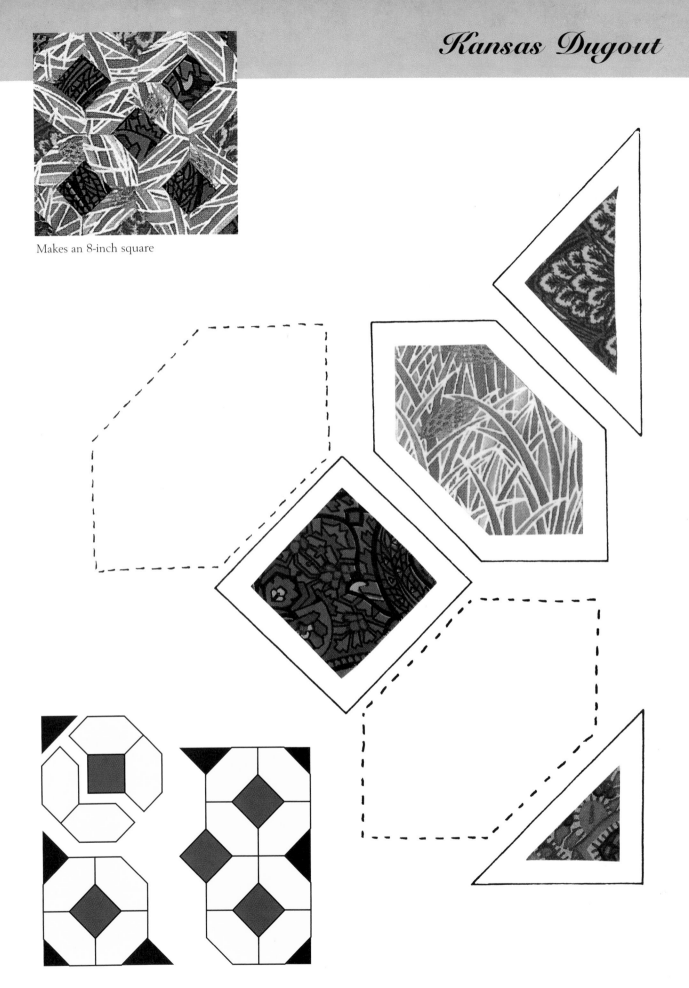

Makes an 8-inch square

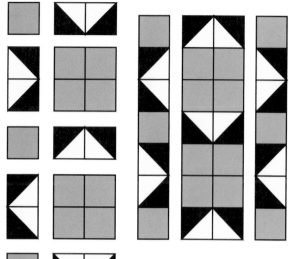

Makes a 14-inch square

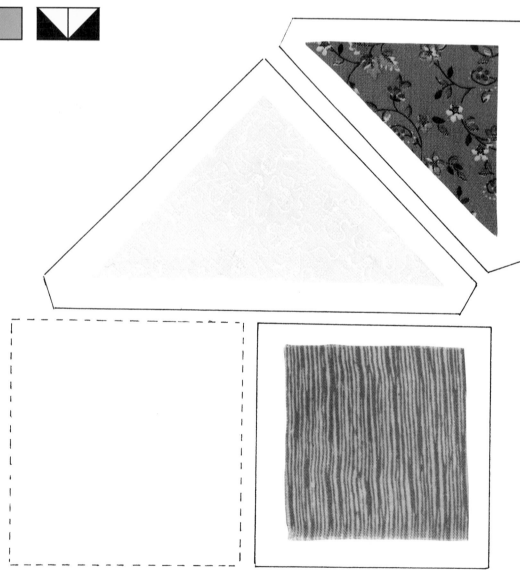

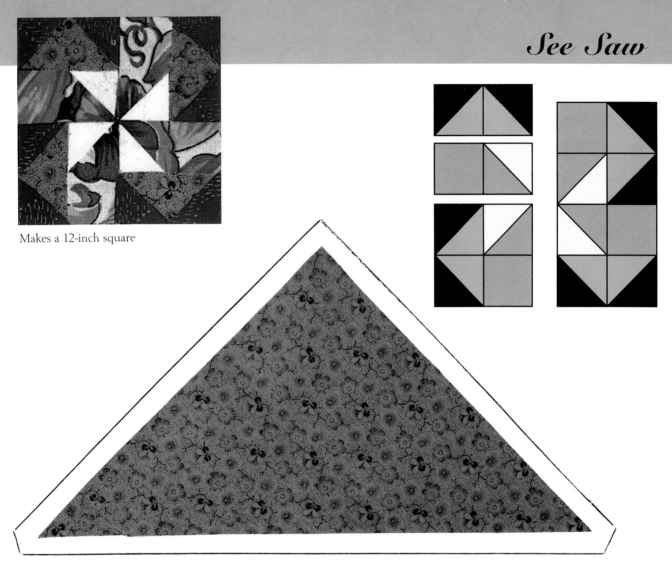

Makes a 12-inch square

Storm at Sea

Makes a 14-inch square

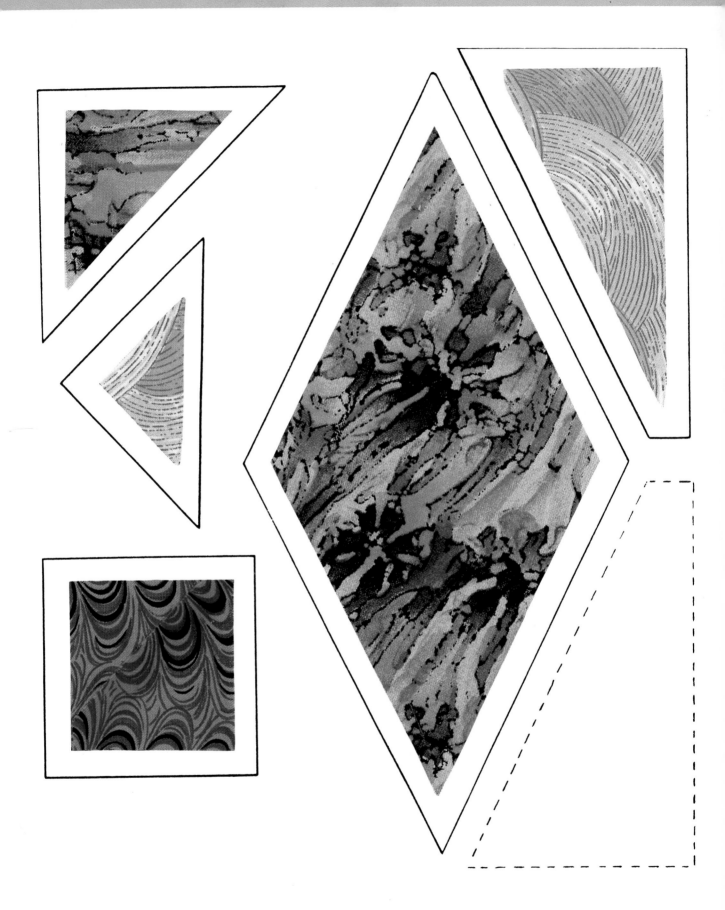

Makes a 12-inch square

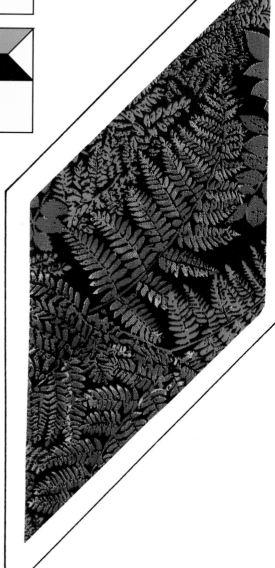

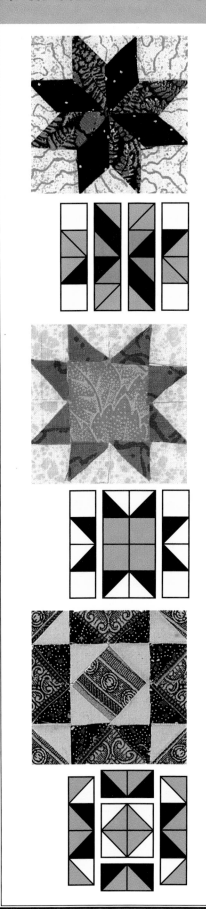

Makes a 12-inch square

Sources

You'll find that most of the quilter's tools that were used to make the projects in this book are available in fabric, craft, and art supply stores, with the possible exception of quilting frames, which are advertised in many quilting magazines.

Dollmaker
Sharon Provost
82 Sandhill Road
Essex, Vermont 05451

Patterns
Folkwear, Inc.
The Taunton Press
63 South Main Street - Box 5506
Newtown, Connecticut 06470-5506

Sunprinting Chemicals
Gramma's Graphics, Inc.
20 Berling Gap - Department MGRU-P4
Fairport, New York 14450
Send $1 and a large, self-addressed stamped envelope for information.

Bibliography

Beaney, Jan. *The Art of the Needle.* London: Bracken Books, 1993.

Benson, Jeanne. *The Art and Technique of Appliqué.* McLean, Virginia: E.P.M. Publications, Inc., 1991.

Beyer, Jinny. *The Quilter's Album of Blocks and Borders.* McLean, Virginia: E.P.M. Publications, 1980.

——. *Medallion Quilts.* McLean, Virginia: E.P.M. Publications, Inc., 1982.

Crow, Nancy. *Nancy Crow: Quilts and Influences.* Paducah, Kentucky: American Quilter's Society, 1990.

Fanning, Bobbie and Tony. *The Complete Book of Machine Quilting.* Radnor, Pennsylvania: Chilton Book Company, 1980.

Goldstein, Nathan. *Painting: Visual and Technical Fundamentals.* Englewood Cliffs, New Jersey: Prentice-Hall, Inc., 1979.

Hall, Carolyn Vosburg. *Pictorial Quilts.* Radnor, Pennsylvania: Chilton Book Company, 1993.

Hall, Jane, and Dixie Haywood. *Perfect Pineapples.* Martinez, California: C&T Publishing, 1989.

Itten, Johannes. *The Art of Color.* New York: Van Nostrand Reinhold Company, 1973.

McDowell, Ruth B. *Pattern on Pattern.* San Francisco: The Quilt Digest Press, 1991.

McMorris, Penny, and Michael Kile. *The Art Quilt.* San Francisco: The Quilt Digest Press, 1986.

Montano, Judith. *The Crazy Quilt Handbook.* Lafayette, California: C&T Publishing, 1986.

Mosey, Caron L. *Contemporary Quilts From Traditional Designs.* New York: E.P. Dutton, 1988.

Smith, Lois. *Fun and Fancy: Machine Quiltmaking.* Paducah, Kentucky: American Quilter's Society, 1989.

Stoner, Charles, and Henry Frankenfield, editors. *Speedball Textbook for Pen and Brush Lettering.* Twentieth Edition. Philadelphia: Hunt Manufacturing Co., 1972.

Wolfrom, Joen. *Landscapes and Illusions.* Lafayette, California: C&T Publishing, 1990.

Index

Page numbers in *italic* refer to photographs and illustrations